Guide to
Vietnam

John R. Jones

BRADT PUBLICATIONS, UK
HUNTER PUBLISHING, USA

First published in 1989 by Bradt Publications, 41 Nortoft Rd, Chalfont St Peter, Bucks SL9 OLA, England. Distributed in the USA by Hunter Publishing Inc., 300 Raritan Center Parkway, CN 94 Edison, NJ 08810.

British Library Cataloguing in Publication Data
Jones, John R.
  Guide to Vietnam.
  1. Vietnam–Visitors' guides
  I. Title
  915.97'0444

ISBN0-946983-36-4

Maps by Hans van Well
Photos by the author
Drawings by Jane Keay

Typeset by Irish Typesetting & Publishing Co. Ltd., Galway, Ireland.
Printed and Bound in Great Britain by
The Guernsey Press Co. Ltd., Guernsey, Channel Islands.

This book is dedicated to Lan Hinh, Nguyen Duy Hoai and all my friends in Vietnam.

The Author

John R Jones is a professional travel photographer and biologist. He has contributed photographs for publications worldwide, his varied assignments taking him to over 50 countries. He is the author of *Vietnam Now* a photographic coverage of the country published by Aston Publications.

Acknowledgements

Immeasurable thanks must go to Lan Hinh without whose help this guide would not have been possible. Nguyen Duy Hoai deserves a special mention for his assistance and friendship throughout. The Vietnam Tourist Authority was tremendously supportive; a special thanks must go to all the interpreters concerned in the various provinces and my drivers Cuong, Minh, Hoanh and Hung who were extremely efficient during every stage of the journey.

Alison deserves credit for her patience and understanding during the writing of this book.

I would like to thank Jane Keay for her excellent drawings from my photographs which have added considerable interest to the guide.

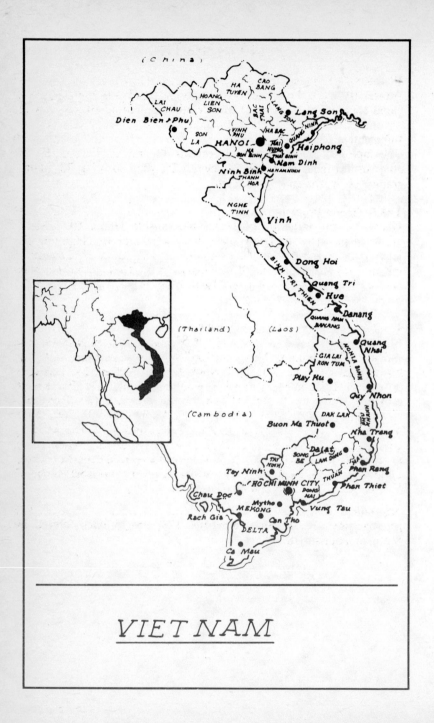

VIET NAM

CONTENTS

INTRODUCTION

Thousands of tourists are now visiting Vietnam from all over the world. I hope this guide will at least help some of them.

Vietnam lies in the intertropical zone stretching along the eastern border of Indochina. Since the time of the earliest civilisations it has faced countless insurrections which have brought devastating human suffering and dissipation of material resources. Few countries have received more publicity but many people are still unaware that it is one of the most breathtakingly beautiful countries in the East. The north has predominantly a jagged karstic relief, the limestone hills and mountains being reminiscent of southern China. Subtropical vegetation flourishes in the temperate subtropical regions and provides sites for famous recreational centres at Dalat in the South, Bach Ma in the centre and Ba Vi in the North. The natural beauty of the virgin timberlands in the central highlands, the rice granaries of the Red River Delta in the North and Mekong Delta in the South, the sheltered bays such as Ha Long, Cau-Hai and Cam Ranh, and the famous beaches of Vung Tau, Nha Trang, Sam Son and Tra Co are well recorded by Vietnamese poets. To travel through the Cu Mong Pass between Quinhon and Cam Ranh and the Ca Pass to Nha Trang is a richly rewarding experience.

The people are mild mannered, sensitive, tenacious and amongst the most naturally courteous, friendly and hospitable to be found in any part of the globe. They have a tough perseverance and intensively courageous attitude which has helped them to rebuild the country, not only structurally but also morally, culturally, medically and educationally. These people, who have survived indiscriminate bombings, yellow rain and napalm, are exceptionally proud of their country. Thousands of bomb craters have been filled in, marshes are being drained, dams and irrigation schemes are being built, and hydroelectric power stations are sprouting up. The scars are still there but they are more concealed in people's hearts than being visible in the landscapes.

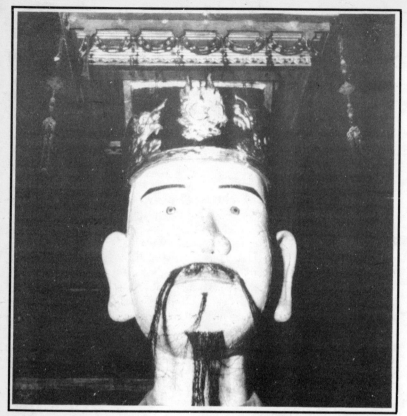

King Dinh Bo Linh

Vietnam–The Country

A Brief History

Remains of prehistoric man have been found in Vietnam dating from the paleolithic age, 300,000–500,000 years ago. By the neolithic age (10,000 years ago) he was well established. During the second millennium BC the Hung kings ruled and their kingdom, Van Lang, became known as Au Lac. For the next 1,000 years, from 111 BC, Vietnam was taken over by the Han and became part of the southern Chinese empire. Revolutionaries during this period, the Trung sisters (40–43 AD), Vietnam's answer to Joan of Arc, Trieu Au (248) with the enormous hanging breasts, and the Black Emperor Mai Thuc Loan (722), attempted to rid the country of Chinese oppression.

Well remembered are Duong Dinh Nghe's struggle against the southern Han (931) and the battle of Ba Chi Dan river in 938. The immortal heroes King Dinh Bo Linh and his successor Le Hoan, from their capital at Hoa-Lu rallied enormous peasant armies to ward off Chinese and Cham invaders.

During the Ly dynasty (1010–1225) the border of Vietnam stretched only as far as the southern end of Nghe Tinh province today. South of this point was the "Kingdom of Champa" ruled by the Cham people.

Confucianism was the dominant religion with its cult temple, the 'Temple of Literature' being its focal point in the old capital of Thang Long (now Hanoi). The period that followed showed a strong Buddhist uprising during which pagodas were built and prayer bells were cast. National feeling strengthened when Ly Thuong Kiet defeated the Chinese. A magnificent victory by Tran Hung Dao, the 'Prince of the restored virtue' against the mighty armies of Kublai Khan followed during the Tran dynasty (1225–1400). The people of Vietnam were adamant that although they were a small nation they could, if required, muster up a punch hard enough to defeat even the might of the Mongol empire.

During the second Tran dynasty (1407–1427) Ming invasions began and many works of art were destroyed. The brilliant strategists Le Loi and Nguyen Trai, from a base in what is now Nghe Tinh province, struck hard and regained independence for Dai Vet.

The border of Vietnam was extended southwards during the reign of King Le Thanh Tong deep into the heart of the 'Kingdom of Champa'.

A period followed in the second Le dynasty (1533–1788) when a civil war raged between the Trinh Lords in the north and the Nguyen Lords in the south. The mandarins had exploited the peasants for years and in the 18th Century they rose up in a great rebellion. The movement which became known as the Tay Son, was led by Nguyen Hue who defeated both the Trinh and the Nguyen despite their massive reinforcements. The regime finally ended in 1802 when Gia Long ascended the throne in the ancient imperial capital of Vietnam, Hue.

By this time, Champa had fallen and its last king fled to Cambodia. Vietnam now extended to 1,500 miles of coastline. A quick succession of 13 Nguyen Kings followed during the period 1802–1945. The Nguyen dynasty was plagued with endless peasant riots and when the French attacked in 1858 there was very little resistance by the Vietnamese. Saigon fell to the French in 1861 and by 1883 during Kien Phuc's rule, the French dominance of Vietnam was at its height. The country was then divided into Tonkin — the Red River delta, Annam — the central area, and Cochinchina to the south.

The fight for independence was tough during the years 1883–1945, but even the tactics of the imperial censor Phan Dinh Phung and Phan Boi Chau were not enough. In 1940 Nguyen Ai Quoc, alias Ho Chi Minh, set the course for future independence by forming the League for the Independence of Vietnam called the Viet Minh. The Japanese invaded in 1941 and overthrew the French. After the surrender of the Japanese in August 1945, the Democratic Republic of Vietnam was formed under the leadership of Ho Chi Minh. This independence was only short lived, however, and the French, after gaining control in the south, retook Tonkin in July 1947. A period of intense resistance followed culminating in the fierce battle of Dien Bien Phu (1954).

The French were defeated by Giap's army and on July 20 1954 the Geneva Agreement was signed, ending the Indochina war, and dividing the country at the 17th parallel. North Vietnam was under communist rule, receiving aid from China, and South Vietnam was governed by Dinh Diem, nominated in June 1954 by emperor Bao Dai, and supported by the West.

The United States, under President Kennedy, set up the Military Assistance Command in Saigon in 1962 to preserve the pro-West independence of the South and by extension the rest of Indochina (the 'domino theory'). He increased military aid in 1963, and after Kennedy's assassination President Johnson stepped up support for the South against incursions by the Viet Minh, known in South Vietnam as Vietcong (rebels). The Gulf of Tonkin incident in August 1964, when two US destroyers were reportedly attacked by North Vietnamese torpedo boats, further increased tensions and discussions took place between Dean Rusk and Robert McNamara on the possibility of bombing the North; this plan was, at that time, opposed by Johnson.

The second Indochina war, known in the West as the Vietnam War, and in Vietnam as the American War, began in earnest in March 1965, when the US put Operation Rolling Thunder into action with the bombing of targets in North Vietnam. The first American troops set foot on Vietnamese soil at Danang on March 8. Throughout the year the US increased their military strength, and by the end of 1966 there were over 400,000 Americans fighting in Vietnam.

Diem's rule in South Vietnam was followed by a series of crisis cabinets until 1967 when President Nguyen Van Thieu was elected.

After initial successes by the South when the combined strength of the American and South Vietnamese armies wiped out entire divisions of North Vietnamese, the highly motivated troops and guerrillas from the North inflicted heavy casualties; by the end of 1965 an average of 1,000 Americans a month were being killed. Then in May 1967 Operation Junction City took 3,000 Vietcong lives and victories in the Mekong delta and central highlands gave America the impression that victory was in sight. The Tet Offensive in 1968 put paid to that illusion, with attacks on many provincial and district capitals in the South. By the end of March the bombing of the North had been discontinued, and in 1969 the Nixon administration began to withdraw troops, relying on money, weapons, and air-support to aid the South Vietnamese army. Towards the end of 1969 massive anti-war demonstrations were held in America, and in the same year Ho Chi Minh, one of the greatest revolutionary leaders of all time, died in Hanoi.

North Vietnam was again bombed in 1970, along with Laos and Cambodia, and, after further successful North Vietnamese offensives into the South, Hanoi and Haiphong were heavily bombed in December.

Negotiations between Henry Kissinger and Le Duc Tho led to a cease-fire being signed in Paris on January 27 1973. The Nobel Peace Prize was jointly awarded to the two negotiators, but not accepted by Le Duc Tho. By March 30 the last American troops had left Vietnam.

During the eight years of war, the United States dropped seven million tonnes of bombs on Vietnam and sprayed 16,200 square kilometres of land with defoliants. A total of 2,800,000 Americans served there, and 57,000 were killed; two million Vietnamese (from both sides) died.

Despite the International Control Commission set up after the cease fire, the fighting continued with the North consolidating its gains in the South. In April 1975 the evacuation of the remaining Americans (mostly journalists) and their families from the Tan Son Nhut airbase was made amid scenes of chaos as crowds of South Vietnamese personnel fought desperately to board the helicopters reserved only

for Americans. The evacuation of the American Embassy was delayed
by bad weather until April 30, only hours before the North Vietnamese tanks crashed through the gates of the Presidential Palace in the
final stages of the invasion/liberation of the South.

In July 1976 the reunited country was named The Socialist Republic
of Vietnam, and Saigon renamed Ho Chi Minh City.

The Economy

War, famine and overpopulation have considerably affected economic
development. Since the liberation of the South in 1975 Socialist
policies have been applied throughout the country.

The North has abundant mineral resources, particularly coal, and
many large industries, while the South relies chiefly on agriculture.
The restoration of the economy in the North was largely accomplished
during 1976 but in the South a more complex situation has existed.
Immediately after the Vietnam War the removal of American aid led
to the closure of many light industries. There was unemployment,
famine and increased black market activities which produced rapid
inflation. Since 1976 things have improved, more jobs have been
created, materials are more readily available and more peasants have
returned to the land.

There has been a long term industrial expansion policy implemented, better management of agriculture and better exploitation of
resources. The country is however still dependent on aid from the
Soviet Union.

The People

There are 54 ethnic groups living in Vietnam. The main one,
accounting for 90% of the population, is the Viet. The 53 others total
about 5.5 million people. How to visit some of these minorities is dealt
with later. The main groups are listed below:

Austro-Asian family
Meo-Zao language group   Hmong (Meo), Pathen, Zao

Tay-Thai language group   Thai, Lao, Lu, Boy, Nung, Tay, San
Chay, Giay

Mon-Khmer language group   Khmer, K'hor, Hre, Chor, Ta Oi,
Cho Ro, Odu, Ma, Ta Oi, Mang, Ro Mam, O Du, Bru-Van Kieu,
Sedang, Bahnar, Hre, Co Tu, Mnong, Brau, Khang, Kho Mu, Gie-
Trieng, Stieng, Chor, Xinh Mun

Viet-Munong language group   Viet, Muong, Chut, Tho

Other language groups   La Ha, Pu Peo, Co Lao, La Chi

Sino-Tibetan family
Tibeto-Burmese language group   Ha Nhi, La Hu, Coong, Si La, Lo Lo, Phu La

Chinese language group   Hoa, San Ziu, Ngai

If you want detailed information on minority people in Vietnam, you should read:
Ethnic Minorities in Vietnam published by the Foreign Language Publishing House, Hanoi.
The Socialist Republic of Vietnam by the same publishers which has an excellent chapter on minority people.

Religion
Catholicism
The first Catholic mission to be set up in Vietnam was in 1615. By 1631 their activities had been suppressed in the South and by 1661 in the North also. Their numbers increased during French rule, but after the signing of the Geneva Agreement and the splitting of Vietnam into North and South in 1954 many in the North fled for their lives. It was a new age of prosperity for Catholics during Diem's rule when their numbers in the South swelled to over 2 million. Diem, himself a Catholic, had many appointed to senior posts in the Government and Army. After the unification of Vietnam freedom of religion became a thing of the past and Catholics fled the country.

Cao Dai sect
This strange religious sect was founded in 1926 by Nguyen Van Chieu and Pham Cong Tac. Its main principles are God, humanity and justice. It is really a mixture of religions: Buddhism, Catholicism, Taoism and Confucianism. The headquarters of this sect is at Tay Ninh. Miniatures of the Tay Ninh Cathedral are seen all over the Mekong area all having in common a large ever-seeing eye placed in a prominent position on the front of the building and on the main altar. The religion rapidly developed into a political organisation opposed to French rule in Vietnam.

Buddhism
A variety of theories say that Buddha was born in the year 563 BC. According to ancient manuscripts Buddhism originated in Vietnam during the first century after Christ. From the 10th Century onwards it was the dominant religion. During the 13th Century the rulers acquired Buddhist monk advisers. Many of the important Buddhist architectural masterpieces were built between the 10th and 15th Centuries. During the 16th Century many of the rulers lost interest in Buddhism when it was rebuked by Confucian* scholars. After a

temporary setback it increased in popularity and today it is the most
popular religion in Vietnam.

Confucianism

This originated in Vietnam during the first century of the Christian era
and was the dominant religion during the 1,000 years when China first
ruled Vietnam. Confucius (551–479 BC) whose real name was Kong
Qiu, started his career as a mandarin. The Temple of Literature
founded in 1070 is dedicated to the cult of Confucius. Over the
centuries his doctrines have been practised widely throughout
Vietnam.

Hoa Hao

This sect was founded in 1939 by the mad monk, Huynh Phu So, in
present day An Giang province in the Mekong Delta. His followers
believed that under 'The Messiah's' guidance they would be able to
build a happy society. As its followers multiplied, the French authorities feared that its strength would increase and so they imprisoned its
leader. 'The Messiah' was released during the Japanese occupation
and popularity of the sect grew. During Diem's rule it suffered
considerably, altars were destroyed and its leaders executed. Although
it made a brief comeback in 1966 its main leader turned rebel and was
imprisoned by the authorities. His followers went into hiding and the
sect gradually disappeared.

Geography

There are three main geographical regions:

The north and northeastern region of Bac Bo

This stretches all the way from the valley of the Red River to the
Chinese border, and includes the whole of the Bac Bo delta. The area
is dominated by low mountain ranges, hills and deep depressions
containing lakes and numerous rivers. The minorities which inhabit
the area grow beans, maize, medicinal plants, fruit trees and raise pigs,
cows and horses. Tea grows well in the uplands and the higher
mountainous regions have massive forests. The Bac Bo plain is
probably the most important area, containing the Red River rice
granaries, the capital Hanoi and the port of Haiphong. Many famous
scenic areas occur in the region Halong Bay, Tra Co beach, Lake Ba
Be and Ban Gioc falls.

The northwestern and northern region of Trung Bo

This extends from the southern mountainous edge of the Bac Bo plain
and the mountains of Bach Ma and Mang as far as the Hai Van Pass
between Hue and Danang. There are many sub-regions.

Hoang Lien Son contains the highest mountain in Vietnam, Fan Si Pan (3143m). The lower areas are famous for the raising of medicinal plants, the breeding of milk cows and exotic flowers. In the northwestern region the limestone peaks of Pu Sam Sao stretch along the Vietnam/Laos border. Here subtropical vegetation flourishes including the very rare To Hap tree. The Cuc Phuong National Park located in the Hoa Binh-Thanh Hoa hilly area is famous for its forests. The sub-region of Nghe Tinh stretches from the Chu river to the Hoanh Son mountain pass. There are many islands offshore. The very wet Binh Tri Thien sub-region extends from the Hoanh Son range of mountains at the Ngang Pass as far as the Hai Van Pass. On its western side the Truong Son range slopes gently towards the Mekong. This geographical area also contains the largest lagoons in Vietnam, Cau Hai and Tam Giang.

Southern Trung Bo and Nam Bo regions
This extends South of the Hai Van Pass. It includes the mountains of Kon Tum and the main port of Danang. Dense forests containing cinnamon occur over 1000m. Coconut tree plantations, now recovered from war damage, reach from Bong Son to Tam Quan. The Tay Nguyen area is known for its schistic and basaltic soils which are excellent for the growth of tea, coffee and rubber. Rich fishing beds are seen off Binh Dinh and Phu Yen. Beyond the Ca Pass is the Southern Trung Bo with the hilly plateau district of Dalat, the beautiful coastal area of Khanh Hoa, the salt marshes of Ca Na and the fishing port of Phan Thiet. The Eastern Nam Bo is noted for its agriculture, particularly the growing of ground nuts, sugar cane and tobacco in the Tay Ninh and Dong Nai regions. Between the Eastern and Western Nam Bo is Ho Chi Minh City. To the south are the deltas of the Mekong and Vam Co, an area of Western Nam Bo rich in fishing products, fruit trees, mangrove forests and Vietnam's largest rice growing area.

Climate And When To Travel
There are regional variations throughout the country. In general rain falls between May and November in the South and between April and October in the North. The period of heaviest rainfall is July and August in the North and June, July and September in the South. Humidity is highest in the North in March, April and August and in the South during July, September and October. April is the hottest month in the South (around 35°C).

The most pleasant time to travel in Vietnam is from January to March when rainfall is very low, temperature is about 30°C in the South with low humidity, and in the North much colder (22°C) with high humidity. If you prefer continuous sunshine go to the North around March, but it is never guaranteed.

Architecture

Some of the architecture is undoubtedly influenced by Vietnam's occupation by China for over 1,000 years. Temples, pagodas and sanctuaries are normally built of wood; bamboo often features strongly. Few walls separate interior apartments because of the tropical climate. Chinese influence is strong in the style of the citadels in Co-Loa and Hoa-Lu. That of Long-Thanh built on the site of the Dai-La fortifications and the remains of Tay-Do in Thanh Hoa are evidence of Chinese influence up to the Ho Dynasty. The buildings in the Imperial City are influenced by French style but with a dominance of Vietnamese originality. Many of the buildings in Ho Chi Minh and Hanoi are typically French.

The visitor will notice that certain animals feature stongly in temple architecture:

The Tortoise (Quy) — The symbol of long life. In Confucian temples the tortoise often has a crane on its back, this also symbolises longevity.

The Phoenix (Phuong) — The symbol of peace and prosperity. To the Vietnamese it is a very celestial bird: the head symbolises the sky, the back the moon, the wings the wind, the eyes the sun, the tail the planets and the feet the earth.

The Unicorn (Ly) — The symbol of intelligence and goodness. The Vietnamese believe that a unicorn appeared when Confucius was born (481 BC).

The Dragon (Long) — The symbol of the Emperors and immortality.

Culture

The number of regional festivals in Vietnam is astonishing. During these there are often singing performances, Trong Quan and water puppet shows. Occasionally there is a festival of mountainous regions, when a large variety of ethnic minorities perform traditional dances and songs. There are even theatrical festivals during which there are performances of popular theatre — Cheo, and Tuong — classical opera. Vietnam has a Ministry of Culture which regularly holds courses for training students in theatrical activities. The songs and dances of minority people are being revived.

Many festivals occur right throughout Vietnam but most occur in the North. Those in central and southern provinces are dealt with under the appropriate sections.

Major festivals and holidays

Tet   Occurs throughout Vietnam (see description under festivals in the North).

Ram Thang Gieng   This is a Buddhist festival occurring on the 15th day of the first lunar month. This is the most important celebration of the Buddhist year.

March 8th   This is National Women's Day when there are parades in most cities.

Easter   Some Catholics celebrate this, particularly in the South.

April 12th   Anniversary commemorating the Emperor Hung Vuong, the first King of Vietnam.

May 1st   Labour Day, a public holiday celebrated on the full moon day of the fourth lunar month. Temples and pagodas are decorated with lanterns.

May 15th   Buddha's birthday.

June 1st   Children's Day.

July — August   Wandering Souls' Day falls on the full moon day of the seventh lunar month. Offerings of food and gifts are made at homes and temples for the wandering souls of the forgotten dead.

September — October   The mid-autumn festival falls on the full moon day of the eighth lunar month. Moon cakes are sold and colourful lanterns are hung by children in temples.

September 2nd   Independence Day. There are marches and parades.

November 20th   Teachers' Day when school children present flowers to their teacher.

December 25th   Christmas.

Festivals in the North

Every traveller likes to get as much for his money as possible and for this reason it is a good idea to time a visit to Vietnam to correspond with major festivals. An indication of the most important festivals in the North is given below. If you want to visit a festival, a request must be sent through to the tourist authority in Hanoi three months before your visit with your requested itinerary. Contact Vietnam Tourism, 54 Nguyen Du Street, Hanoi SRV, Tel 54674–55963, Telex 4269–4552 Tourism VT. I have heard of tourists just arriving and being successful but it is the exception rather than the rule — so be warned!

Undoubtedly the most spectacular of all in the North is The Huong Tich Festival. In my opinion this is even more fascinating than the Tet Festival. To get to Huong Tich is not easy. It is best to rely on Vietnam Tourism which will provide a driver and an interpreter. Huong Tich is the name of a low mountain range 50 km west of Hanoi. The area has many picturesque grottoes, pagodas and temples which draw tens of

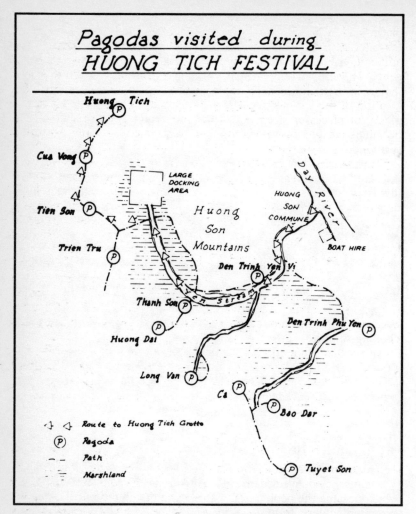

Pagodas visited during HUONG TICH FESTIVAL

Huong Tich

Cua Vong

LARGE DOCKING AREA

Huong Son Mountains

Day River

HUONG SON COMMUNE

BOAT HIRE

Tien Son

Trien Tru

Den Trinh Yen Vi

Thanh Son

Den Trinh Phu Yen

Huong Dai

Long Van

Ca

Bao Dar

Tuyet Son

Route to Huong Tich Grotto

(P) Pagoda

- - Path

Marshland

thousands of pilgrims from all parts of the country every spring. As a tourist attraction it is even equal to a visit to Halong Bay in the Tonkin Gulf. The best time to visit is the middle of the first lunar month.

A one hour drive from Hanoi takes you across the Day River, a tributary of the Red River, to Huong Son Commune. Here a boat may be hired which will transport you along the Yen Stream past remarkable karst mountains with peculiar names such as the Crouching Elephant, the Nun, the Rice Tray and the Bronze. It is useful if you take the trouble to learn a little Vietnamese, 'A di da phat' (may Buddha bless you) is the traditional greeting used from one pilgrim to another. The Huong Son range of mountains where the festival takes place is probably the most spectacular scenery in Vietnam, equal to that at Guillin in southern China. Unless you spend one week in the area you will not see all the pagodas because some are very difficult to get to. However in only one day you will see Huong Tich grotto where the main festivities take place. To give the tourist an idea of the location of the various pagodas a simple map is provided. There are plenty of places to sleep out in the mountains because shelters are provided for the enormous number of people who come to spend several days in the area.

The Huong Tich grotto is reached from the large docking area indicated on the map. It is a long walk up the mountain along winding flights of stone steps. There are refreshments en route and large numbers of resting places. Don't take too much gear along with you (special warning to photographers) as it is a tough climb. Inside the grotto, stalactites and stalagmites of all sizes gleam mysteriously in the joss-stick smoke-filled atmosphere. There are a variety of small shrines in the cave together with a huge banner — the symbol of Huong Tich.

Warning: devout pilgrims usually go to Huong Tich very early in spring, long before the peak season. If you leave it too late in spring the paths are crammed with Vietnamese tourists and the grotto, because of the enormous amount of incense burnt, will be filled with choking smoke.

An excellent time to visit Huong Tich is around the time of the Lac Long Quan Festival held from the first to the sixth day of the third lunar month at Binh Minh village, Than Oai district, Ha Son Binh province. This village is on the way to the Huong Son commune. Allow at least two days if you want to visit both.

The Lac Long Quan Festival

The festival, which is dedicated to Lac Long Quan, begins with the Le Te Ceremony. Lac Long Quan is regarded to be the ancestor of the Vietnamese people since his wife, Au Co, produced one hundred eggs which became the people of the Delta and the mountains. During the ceremony elders from the village, dressed in silk costumes, pay homage in front of a very colourful altar. Traditional music is played and flowers, wine and gifts are presented by the villagers of Binh Minh to the Buddha. A spectacular procession of young ladies transporting altars loaded with fruit and colourful flowers follows the narrow streets of Binh Minh. Firework displays and often dragon dances are performed.

Tet Festival

This occurs all over Vietnam. Tet is the first day of the lunar year. The Vietnamese people call the transition from one year to another the Giao Thua. The day before Tet is the time for the Ta Nien Ceremony in which sacrifices are given to the Buddha. It is a time of great rejoicing. A tourist wishing to visit Vietnam during Tet should make arrangments at least four months in advance. The hotels in Hanoi and Ho Chi Minh city are completely full during this period and nobody should attempt to arrive without prior reservation. There have been reports of tourists flying in from Manila, where the Vietnamese visa facilities are said to be lax, and finding it impossible to get accommodation anywhere, some unfortunates have found themselves on the next plane out. It is worth the trouble of booking in advance because Tet is indeed a joyous occasion. The best place to visit during Tet is undoubtedly Hanoi. The noise of countless fire crackers begins even before the first day of Tet. The flower stalls in the old part of Hanoi are a sight to behold. Every household is decorated with flowers. It is still possible in parts of Hanoi to see the Cay Neu — this is a bamboo pole with a small basket on top containing areca nuts, betel and a small square of woven bamboo. The structure is supposed to ward off evil spirits. Lime dust scattering outside the house is a further custom still practised to give Buddha's protection against the evil spirits. The timing of the Tet Festival at the beginning of the spring equinox is important in an agricultural nation because this is a period in which people can enjoy life. The Ta Nien Ceremony on the eve of Tet invites the deceased members of the family to return and partake in the life of their descendants. Firecrackers are let off in their thousands during the Tet period. This custom was performed originally to scare off the wicked spirits of Na Ong and his wife Na Ba who hated everyone. They were so bitter in their hatred that they always played nasty tricks on their fellows. Nowadays the firecrackers delight the children who try to make as much noise as possible. On the morning of Tet families hope that their first visitor will be a happy person because this will give them good luck throughout the next year. During Tet everyone should be friendly with everyone else. Vietnamese people are the most friendly you could meet anywhere, but during Tet their hospitality and warm nature is second to none. A very photogenic activity which is performed during Tet is the Dragon Dance when the performers harmoniously undulate the dragon into vivacious energetic movements, performing from under the belly of the beast. It originates from the Rong Ran — the Dragon snake game which can be seen played in many playgrounds throughout Vietnam. The fourth day is the end of Tet. The Cay Neu is not generally taken down until the seventh day after Tet.

The New Year is a good time to visit Hanoi as there are many other festivals which take place at this time.

Dong Da festival
This occurs in the Dong Da district of Hanoi on the fifth day of the first lunar month. It commemorates the fighters who died in the battle

against the Sing in 1789 under the leadership of King Quang Trung — the leader of the Tay Son rebellion.

Mai Dong festival

This takes place at Mai Dong temple, Hai Ba Trung district, Hanoi from the fourth to the sixth day of the first lunar month. This festival pays homage to Lady Le Chan, a renowned and brave female general of the two Trung sisters' army who fought against the Chinese (40–43 AD). There is generally a good wrestling match during this festival.

An Duong Vuong festival

Taking place at An Duong Vuong temple in Co Loa village, Dong Anh district in the suburb of Hanoi. This is easily reached by bicycle from Hanoi by way of the Soaring Dragon Bridge. It begins on the sixth and ends on the sixteenth day of the first lunar month. It commemorates Thuc Phan, one of the founders of ancient Vietnam four thousand years ago.

Ha Loi festival

Occurs at Ha Loi temple in the Me Linh suburb of Hanoi. It falls on the fifteenth day of the first lunar month. It commemorates the two Trung sisters who led the uprising against Chinese aggressors in 40–43 AD. During the course of the festival, games and entertainments are held. The ceremony of offering *Banh Troi* is one of the remarkable events. This is a kind of cake made up of sticky rice dough, which is wrapped around a piece of diced brown sugar.

Den Va Temple festival

In Bat Bat suburb of Hanoi the festival occurs on the fifteenth day of the first lunar month. It is dedicated to Tan Vien, God of the Mountain, who is said to be of a higher status than the God of the Sea. He wins a battle to be the King's son-in-law. A spectacular battle between the God of the Mountain and the God of the Sea occurs during the festivities.

The other festivals in the North are more difficult to get to than those already considered. Ha Bac province is especially known for its festivals, but it should be stressed that Vietnam Tourism must be informed at least four months before if a tourist wants to visit any of these festivals. Few westerners have ever visited the festivals in Ha Bac province and it is quite likely that requests through the Tourist Authority which are passed onto higher authorities will be refused. For those who would like to attempt it, here is a list of the festivals in Ha Bac province. There is only one way a westerner will get to the festival areas and that is by car with a driver and interpreter.

Dong Ky festival

Occurring on the fifteenth day of the first lunar month in Dong Ky village, Tien Son district, Ha Bac province. This commemorates Thien

Cuong De, who successfully fought against Xich Quy during the Hung Kings period — 4,000 years ago. There is a firecracker competition held during the festival. This is the biggest and most spectacular festival in the area.

Smaller local festivals are also held in the province.

Van Village festival   In Viet Yen district from the seventeenth to the twentieth day of the first lunar month.

Tho Ha Village festival   Viet Yen district from the twentieth to the twenty second day of the first lunar month.

De Tham festival   In Yen-The district on 16th March.

Dau Temple festival   In Thuan Thanh district on 8th April.

But Thap festival   In Thuan Thanh district on the twenty third day of the third lunar month.

Suoi Mo Temple festival   In Luc-Nam district on the second lunar month.

Vietnam is indeed a nation for festivals for there are many more which occur in the North. Other interesting festivals are: **Le Phung Hieu Temple festival** This starts on the seventh day of the first lunar month at Le Phung Hieu temple in Hoang Hoa district, Thanh Hoa province. The Tourist Authority can easily arrange for you to visit this festival providing you give them advance warning. They will provide a car and driver and interpreter to take you through a really scenic area in Ha Nam Ninh province on the journey down to this area festival. Although it is only a local festival, it's really considered to be a big popular event by the people living in neighbouring areas. The festival is dedicated to Le Phung Hieu, a general of Ly Dynasty (11th Century). There are competitions for the best sticky rice cake.

Another fairly easy festival to get permission to visit is **Binh Da festival** in Binh Da, Ha Son Binh province. This is from the sixth day of the third lunar month. The festivities include firecracker competitions, folk singing and many traditional games.

Another in the same region is the **Thay Pagoda festival** in Quoc Oai, Ha Son Binh province, which occurs on the seventh day of the third lunar month. This is dedicated to To Dao Hanh, a revered Buddhist monk and teacher. It features water puppet shows, boat rowing contests and mountain climbing.

A difficult festival to get permission to visit is **The Khuc Lac and Di Nau festival** which occurs in Tam Nong district, Vinh Phu province, and happens on the seventh and twenty sixth day of the first lunar month. It is a festival in which people pray for good luck.

A very interesting festival which the Tourist Authority will only be too glad to take overseas visitors to is the **Den festival**. This occurs in Hanamninh province at the site of the ancient capital of Vietnam at Hoa Lu. It takes place on 12th March and is a mixture of two festivals. These are the Dinh Bo Linh festival and the Le King festival named after the King Dinh Bo Linh and General Le who fought off insurrection attempts by Sung invaders. During the Den, activities including fighting with reed flags are performed in which performers demonstrate a game with reeds popularised by King Dinh.

It is well worth visiting this festival since there are other attractions on offer in this area (see relevant chapter).

Water puppetry
This deserves a special mention since it is only seen in Vietnam.

Where to see it   The only certain place to see a water puppet show is at the Thay Pagoda festival in Quoc Oai district, Ha Son Binh province on the seventh day of the third lunar month. Various guilds perform in this festival including Dao Thuc, Nhan Tai and Thi Lan from Dong Anh district, Hanoi and Phu Da and Trang Son from Thach That district, Hanoi. There are also reports of water puppet shows at Trang Son and Giong Temple, Hanoi.

History   There is evidence that such shows occurred as early as the 8th Century. By the Ly dynasty it was well developed, and expanded even more during the Tran (1225–1400). It is regarded as a very old artistic creation of the inhabitants of the Red River delta.

The Puppets   The usual method of manipulation is by rod (*may sao*).
The puppets are made of supple light woods and are coated with
lacquer, and gold and silver foil.

At the Thay pagoda the performance is given in front of the
manipulators' room (*buong tro*) sometimes called the House of
Puppets (*nha roi*). The method of operation from behind is similar to
Japanese *Bunraku*. The manipulators wallow in the water which serves
the same function as a curtain, hiding them — their room is half under
water. The Thuy Dinh permanent theatre at the Thay pagoda is built
out of several bays from which the performers manipulate their
puppets on special rods or using ropes (*may day*).

The show begins when a clown burns the *la xi* incense stick or lets off
a small firecracker, *phao chuot*, kindled in the manipulators' room.
The repertoire is composed of sketches from legends, historic events
and fables. Some troupes use a verbal accompaniment but others
favour percussion instruments, drums, timbals and rattles.

Information for visitors

Travelling to and from Vietnam
Most travellers fly from Bangkok, to which cheap fares are available from all over the world.

Getting to Bangkok
From Europe   The cheapest flights are with Aeroflot, Oman Airlines (around £400 return). With Thai, Philippine and British Airways the price is now around £600 return. Hann Overland can arrange cheap flights Tel: 01 834 7337; Trailfinders (Tel: 01 938 3366) and Wexas (Tel: 01 584 8113) are also a good source of cheap flights.

From North America   From the west coast there are cheap flights with World Airways, China Airways, Thai International and Pan Am, expect to pay about $1000 return. Tel: Oc Tours on 415 348 6300 (in California). From New York expect to pay around the same.

From Asia   There are many flights from Kathmandu, Colombo, Tapei, KL, HK, Singapore, New Delhi and Manila.

From Australia   Cheap fares are available from Sydney at about A$1100 return. Contact Orbit Tours, Sydney Tel: 233–3288.

Flying direct
Flights directly to Vietnam are more expensive (see various tourist programmes for the names of the carriers).

To Hanoi	From Moscow	Tuesday, Thursday, Saturday
	Vientian	Monday, Thursday, Saturday
	Phnompenh	Monday, Tuesday, Thursday
	Berlin	Tuesday
	Prague	Wednesday
	Bangkok	Wednesday
To Ho Chi Minh	From Moscow	Monday
	Phnompenh	Monday, Thursday, Saturday
	Paris	Monday, Thursday, Saturday
	Manila	Wednesday

From Hanoi	To Moscow	Tuesday, Thursday, Saturday
	Vientian	Monday, Thursday, Saturday
	Phnompenh	Monday, Tuesday, Thursday
	Berlin	Wednesday
	Prague	Wednesday
	Bangkok	Wednesday, Friday
From Ho Chi Minh	To Moscow	Wednesday
	Phnompenh	Monday, Thursday, Saturday
	Paris	Monday, Thursday
	Manila	Wednesday

Red Tape

Vietnam is now more accessible, with an increasing number of tourists visiting the country every year. There is still the problem of getting the visa, but it is getting easier. The authorities are still not keen on independent travel; tourists are not allowed to travel by train (except on special steam train tours) or on public buses for long distances. It is quite possible to travel independently around cities and even for short distances outside cities. Some journalists have travelled on public transport but they risked being deported. Some have obtained special permission to travel on the train from Hanoi to Hue but this is the exception rather than the rule.

In Vietnam the tourist authorities have everything completely sewn up. If you want to get around you must:

1) Travel on a group tour from a Western country bookable at inflated prices. Everything is packaged including flights, accommodation, food and transport. Expect to pay around $2500 for a 10 day tour which probably includes three in Bangkok.

2) Travel on a group tour which *you* have organised by getting enough people together, and then following one of the programmes once you have arrived in Vietnam. The tourist authority have 16 programmes which they offer at very reasonable prices (see the back of this book). If you can get enough people together you can travel free!

3) Arrange for individual tours with your own interpreter and driver. This is by far the most enjoyable way of seeing Vietnam with a minimum of hassle.

4) Get a visa and just go. It must, however, be pointed out that it is extremely difficult to get visas without a letter of introduction from the tourist authority in Hanoi or Ho Chi Minh or, in the case of business travellers, a letter from the industrial establishment to be visited in Vietnam. Some people, not strictly business travellers, have managed it.

If you do get a visa, unless you use the tourist authority when you arrive, you won't get far. It is fine if you just want to stay in Hanoi or Ho Chi Minh, but if you try travelling from one to the other overland it's a different story. I would personally take my hat off to anyone who could do it independently! It might be worth pointing out to anyone who was thinking of trying that even war photographers returning to Vietnam now travel on 'group tours'.

Don't let all this put you off because once you arrive it is pure magic. If you don't want to pay inflated prices, read on for what to do to obtain your visa.

Entering Vietnam when not on an organised tour

To obtain a visa when you are not on an organised tour can be difficult. The regulations state clearly that visas can only be issued for group travel or for individuals on business. At the back of this guide I have outlined 16 programmes which are available from Vietnam Tourism. They mostly apply to groups but if you want to enter Vietnam individually and have individual arrangements, then add 30% to the cost for small groups.

If you go to the Vietnam Embassy in your country the first thing they will ask you is, are you on an organised tour? If the answer is no — you have little chance of getting a visa, although I am told that some Scandinavian and German tourists have managed it! I have also heard on the travel grapevine that it is easy to get a visa in the Consulate in Manila. It will save you money if you follow these guidelines:

Write to Vietnam Tourism in Ho Chi Minh or Hanoi — whichever you want to visit first.

54 Nguyen Du, Hanoi, SRV		71 Nguyen Hue
Tel: 54674–52986	or	Ho Chi Minh City. SRV
Telex: 4269 Tourism VT		Tel: 90972–90775–90776
		Telex: 295 Dulivina SG

State what programme you want and ask for a letter that you can take to your embassy. You can save hundreds of dollars doing it this way but it's a big hassle. When you have your letter (arrange to get it about three months before going, if possible) take it to your embassy together with (a) 3 completed application forms, (b) 3 photos, (c) valid passport, and (d) visa fee (£8).

If they are in a good mood you may get a visa on the spot, but this is very unlikely. The Consul will write to Hanoi for confirmation. In around two months you will hear if you have been successful. When it gets near to the time you expect a reply, it's a good idea to pester them a little. When you have your visa, telex Hanoi or Ho Chi Minh stating the time of your arrival and flight number. Don't forget to send a letter stating when you will arrive, two months before you leave for Vietnam, and that you intend using their letter to obtain a visa. It's a lot of hassle but don't be put off. The last time I went I got my visa

approved the afternoon before the next morning flight to Thailand!
Business visitors require a letter of sponsorship from their country of
origin, and one from Vietnam to obtain a visa.

In Britain, applications go to the Embassy of the Socialist Republic
of Vietnam

> 12–14 Victoria Road
> London W8.
> Tel: (01) 937 1912
> Open 9–18.30 Monday — Friday.

Visa extensions inside Vietnam

If you arrive in Vietnam on a group tour, at the end of the tour you can
extend your visa for the length of time you were on the tour. For
example, following a tour of two weeks, you can extend your visa for a
further two weeks, making a total stay of a month.

Arriving with no accommodation booked and no tourist packages
will entitle you to no visa extension. Even if you book a three week
tour direct with Vietnam Tourism you will easily get another three
week extension to your visa.

Immigration and Customs

This is now much easier than it was when tourists started arriving in
1977. You have to fill in an arrival card, be consistent — make sure
your profession is the same as on your passport (even if you have
changed it since the passport was issued). This card is typical of any
arrival card. Take care when it comes to filling in your declaration
form, you must list all your valuables, e.g. watches, cameras, lenses
and even your film. Before you arrive in the country you should count
your currency accurately; you may be subjected to a search because of
the thriving black market in Vietnam. Don't try to hide any dollars —
it is an offence. You should fill in your currency declaration form
carefully, writing the amounts in figures and words. Don't lose it. Get
it stamped officially before you leave the customs area. Professional
photographers arriving in Vietnam for the first time are often worried
about the amount of film they are carrying. Don't try to hide any, there
is no problem at all even if you have a few hundred rolls. They hardly
ever bother to even look at them these days. They are also getting very
carefree about counting money and luggage searches. If you want to
get through customs quickly then follow a foreigner not a Vietnamese.

Imports

You are allowed to take into Vietnam 600 cigarettes, or 100 cigars, or
600 grams of pipe tobacco. There is no problem with importing camera
equipment. Gifts are allowed, but don't be excessive, they may
confiscate them. There is no limit on alcoholic drinks.

Exports
You can export things you have purchased in Vietnam except anti-
ques, for which you will need an export licence from the authorities.

Money
Bring American dollars, in cash, and American Express travellers
cheques. Carry plenty of low denomination dollar bills, they are handy
when you need to pay in dollars for beer, etc., in hotels. If you are
travelling overland for long distances make sure you bring dollars in
cash — many banks in isolated regions won't change travellers cheques
and often you can't change dollars, so do your money changing before
leaving the main town.

When staying in cities don't cash too much at a time or you will be
walking around with parcels of dong!

Credit cards are not accepted in Vietnam.

New dong notes are issued in denominations of 1, 2, 5, 10, 20, 50,
100, 500, and 1000. There are no coins. The new dong replaced the old
dong in September, 1985.

Between 1986 and 1988 the official exchange rate has gone from 11
to the dollar to about 87 to the dollar. That is the bank rate. Cash
dollars changed in hotels fetch nearly five times as much, and far, far
more on the black market. Dealing on the blackmarket (for example,
with pedicab drivers) is, of course, illegal, and will result in your
deportation if you are caught. You may also be ripped off by the
dealer.

Always have your currency declaration form stamped when you
change money.

Costs
The cost of your tour, driver and interpreter is expensive by Vietnamese standards. The tourist authority, if you opt for one of their
programmes, will charge you in American dollars. If you pay in
travellers cheques, there will be a 5% surcharge. If you pay in
American dollar cash, they will scrutinise your money carefully using a
money checker.

Vietnam ranks amongst the poorest countries in the world, the
average wage being about 15,000 dong for an educated person per
month. At the black market exchange rate, this is only about 8 U.S.
dollars. Many people earn far less. If you give a tip to a pedicab driver
of say one dollar, you are giving him the equivalent of a few days'
wages. This explains why there are so many pedicab drivers hovering
around entrances to big hotels.

The tourist authority normally caters for your food requirements
and hotel expenses so you normally won't need much money (unless
you drink a lot of beer!). If you eat in backstreet restaurants, expect to
pay about 2,000 dong because you are a foreigner.

Security

There is virtually no security problem in Vietnam, but it is still wise to take precautions. Carry your money in a money belt or in a pocket with a zip inside your trousers. Remember there are other foreigners about so keep an eye on them. Many hotels do have lock-up facilities for valuable equipment.

Other Useful Facts

Communications

You can telephone most places in the world from Hanoi, there's usually only a delay of about 20 minutes. It works out at about $4 a minute from Hanoi to Britain. From Ho Chi Minh for some reason, it take longer to get through. Telex facilities are available at most large hotels in Hanoi and Ho Chi Minh. Airmail letters take one month to Britain.

Newspapers

There are no newspapers in English published but there are two magazines, *Vietnam* and *The Vietnam Courier*. However, these are difficult to obtain. Books are usually in Vietnamese, many are available in Russian and a few in French and English.

Electricity

110 and 220 volts AC. The voltage in some hotels is very irregular.

Time

G.M.T. + 7 hours.

Language

Vietnamese is the official language, French is spoken quite a lot, Russian and Chinese are spoken by some officials. It's worth noting that the tourist authority have interpreters for most languages.

Radio

It is possible to get the BBC World Service. Fiddle around with the frequencies since reception varies with fixed frequencies at certain times of the day.

Travel

Air   The national airline is Hang Khong.

Ho Chi Minh (Tan Son Nhut airport) is 8 km from the city. Hanoi (Noi Bai airport) is 48 km from the city. There are regular internal flights between the capitals and to Hue and Danang.

Sea   Services run from Japan, Singapore, Hong Kong and Kampuchea. The main ports in Vietnam are Ho Chi Minh, Da Nang, Haiphong and Ben Thuy.

Road There are roads into China, Laos and Kampuchea but it is nearly impossible to get permits to travel on them.

Health
Vaccinations required

You are allowed to enter Vietnam with no vaccination certificates against cholera, typhoid or hepatitis. Those entering from a country where there is yellow fever require a certificate to show they have been vaccinated.

Although not an entry requirement it is advisable (according to the School of Tropical Medicine) to be vaccinated against cholera, typhoid, polio, tetanus, hepatitis A and Japanese encephalitis. Most travellers will have never heard of this. It is carried by mosquitoes and a vaccine is available.

Experienced long haul travellers these days are also vaccinated against rabies and hepatitis (gamma globulin).

Give the Tropical School of Medicine a ring if you are unsure about what to do about vaccinations. Liverpool 051 708 9393 or London 01 636 8636.

Some medical problems

Plague The WHO have reported several outbreaks of this in Vietnam. Avoiding contact with fleas is recommended because they are carriers. A suspected mattress can be sprayed with pyrethrum insect spray, but it is best to use flea powder on your body.

Hepatitis A It is a good idea to have a jab against this because it can be caught by drinking contaminated water and eating vegetables washed in local water. Many hardened travellers who have had repeated vaccinations against hepatitis A have some immunity against it. The dose required varies with the amount of time you are spending in the country so consult your doctor. Avoid revaccinations during your stay because of Aids scare.

Hepatitis B and Aids Both viruses are transmitted through blood products and sexual intercourse. Avoid both, and carry a sterile needle pack (and condoms). See *Medical Kit*.

Rabies This is fairly common in Vietnam so try to avoid dogs. Never run from a savage dog, always stand your ground and scare it off somehow. These days the rabies vaccine is perfectly safe and there are no side effects. It costs about £70 for a full course.

Snake bites Most tourists in Vietnam won't come across any, but if you travel in jungle regions there are 131 poisonous varieties. The deadly *krait* can kill a man within 30 minutes, bamboo vipers are the same vivid green as the vegetation, cobras are common. Vietnamese soldiers during the war carried plants called *daunoc* and *breynia*; the leaves are boiled and usually the remedy is quick acting. Tourists who are bitten should remain calm and get to one of the hospitals listed in this guide as soon as possible. To get the correct antidote it is necessary to take the offender with you, but I don't think many people would actually do this. The best thing is to avoid being bitten by wearing high boots and baggy trousers.

Cuts   Since these take a long time to heal, take a good antiseptic cream, wash well with soap and water, cover by Newskin, followed by a plaster. Villagers in Vietnam use the leaves of *lanterwin* and *mo qua*. If you get a bad cut in a remote area where there are some people, rely on their remedy! Leeches can cause nasty wounds so when you remove them touch them with a hot match rather than just pulling them off.

Diarrhoea   For mild diarrhoea, the best treatment is to drink strong black tea. Kaolin tablets work to a certain extent. Make sure your fluid intake is high otherwise excessive dehydration may result. Some travellers carry other tablets for bad diarrhoea such as Lomotil and Imodium but it is advisable to consult your doctor about this before travelling. Very severe diarrhoea requires hospital treatment (see telephone numbers for hospitals under tourist facilities in each section). Blood in your stool is an indication of amoebic dysentery or stool bacillary dysentery. The best treatment is metronidozole which needs a prescription before you go, so get advice from your doctor if you intend travelling in a very remote area and avoid unboiled untreated water. The Vietnamese people use a plant called *dinh nam* which is boiled and drunk against dysentry. It is an excellent idea to take Rehidrat rehydration packs or, if you don't have these, to consume a solution of salt and sugar which will rehydrate you (see *Medical Kit*). Cholera is one of the worst causes of dehydration; hospital treatment is required.

Safeguards against diarrhoea   Maintain a high degree of personal hygiene, avoid drinking local water, always use bottled water which is readily available in Vietnam, and watch what you eat. Take great care of what you eat in small roadside restaurants, make sure everything is well cooked and don't eat your vegetables raw under any circumstances. Uncooked vegetables have been washed, usually in local water which can contain salmonella bacteria. Most common forms of food poisoning are caused by this organism. The Vietnamese people treat it with a tropaeolum plant concoction.

Medical Kit
A good supply of bandages, plasters and cotton wool.

A bottle of Germolene New Skin made by Beecham's. This gives protection to minor cuts, waterproofing and germproofing them. In hot countries cuts heal very slowly so it is essential to have adequate protection for them.

A pain killer such as codeine phosphate or soluble aspirin.

Tiger Balm which is good for stopping insect bites from itching and comes in handy for minor aches and pains in muscles (can be purchased in Bangkok).

An eye ointment containing chloramphenicol.

Anti-diarrhoea tablets, kaolin for minor upsets and either Imodium or Lomotil for more severe cases. Hardened travellers sometimes have Septrin, a broad spectrum antibiotic for very severe cases. This however requires a prescription so consult your doctor. Isogel is very effective against diarrhoea.

Rehydration packs are extremely useful if you should suffer extreme loss of fluid. A supply of salt and sugar is a good idea if you can't get them. Use one teaspoon of salt to eight of sugar in a litre of water.

A strong antibiotic against dysentery, e.g. ampicillin. This requires a prescription.

A fungicide dust powder for minor fungus infections, e.g. ringworm. A good one is Micronazole.

Clove oil to stop toothache (the Vietnamese use the bark of the mango tree, boiled).

Malarial tablets with supply for six weeks after your visit and two weeks before.

Sterile needles in case you need injections (absolutely essential now because of Aids). A kit can be purchased through MASTA, Tel: 01 631 4408.

Small scissors and tweezers.

Emergency dental kit — now available at £7.50 from most dentists.

Sun screen.

Antiseptic cream.

Water sterilising tablets if you are travelling in remote areas.

Supply of quinine if you are on a long trip in the central highlands or Mekong delta, in case you get malaria.

Don't forget medicine for your special needs if you have a particular ailment. It is unlikely that you will be able to get it in Vietnam.

Other essentials related to general health

1. Insect repellent, Diethyl Toluamide.
2. Flea powder. (It has been reported by the WHO that plague occurs in Vietnam; it is carried by fleas!)
3. Medicated shampoo (carbaryl for lice infestations).
4. Mosquito coils.
5. Vitamin tablets. In some areas of Vietnam the food is extremely bad, but generally you wouldn't need them.

6. Condoms, if you are likely to succumb to temptation in Bangkok or
   Ho Chi Minh City.

What to Bring
Clothes

It is interesting to note that few Vietnamese tourist guides take more
than a pack which is about 12 inches by 12 inches. I can't imagine
western tourists travelling as lightly but if they took the hint they
would be far better off. I would personally recommend: —

3 teeshirts made of cotton.
1 cotton long-sleeved shirt for keeping mosquitoes off in the
evening. Get a zip sewn into a large pocket which must be large
enough for a passport; it's ideal for passing through airports.
3 pairs of cotton socks.
4 underpants (cotton — you can have them tailor-made in Bangkok
with small security pockets in them!).
2 pairs of light cotton baggy trousers with pockets and zips all over.
It's a good idea to have a security pocket made for inside the trousers
which will hold a passport and your money. I also have extremely small
pockets made inside the trouser legs and a long, very thin one under
the belt. It's worth pointing out that you needn't be paranoid about
this in Vietnam since the penalties for stealing from tourists are
extremely high. I use these measures for protection against fellow
travellers!
Light walking shoes, flip-flops for showers, bathing and rainy days.
Some people take a light cagoule or Goretex cagoule. A *small*
umbrella is more useful.
1 warm sweater is sufficient for chilly days in Dalat and Hanoi in the
winter.
1 hat for protection against the sun.

The Vietnamese people are not snappy dressers so don't take a suit or
a tie. A suit would be too hot in most places anyway. I have seen
Japanese tourists trying to look cool in a suit in Ho Chi Minh with
sweat streaming down their faces.

Photography

There is no problem bringing in large quantities of film into Vietnam.
Don't attempt to hide it, put it in a large see-through plastic bag and
hold it up for the customs officials to see. You will have to list your
photographic equipment and the number of films you have. You can
photograph virtually anything except bridges, military installations and
the police.
In Ho Chi Minh city there are camera shops selling modern
equipment at very reasonable prices. They do stock film but generally
it is quite old. Slide film can be bought but it is very expensive. I have

never seen Kodachrome 64 for sale in the country. I have never come across a security problem with valuable equipment. In the more remote areas they will stare at your cameras, but maybe because they have never seen any before.

In the hotel, watch you don't store your cameras near the air conditioning unit, you will get condensation right through them. Many hotels in Mekong territory have an ant problem so keep your equipment away from them. They seem to get everywhere particularly the minute red variety. Put cameras in zip-up bags at night or if you use pouches put these inside home-made fine mesh bags.

Be careful with batteries, humidity affects them so keep spare ones wrapped up in toilet paper. If you have to buy new batteries it's fine in Ho Chi Minh but in Hanoi it's a nightmare and those you get will be very run down. If you are using pesticide aerosol sprays to kill mosquitoes, keep your films in sealed plastic bags. Be careful that you don't expose your film to high temperatures, you can ruin them. Take care where you put your film when travelling. Vietnam Tourism don't use air-conditioned cars and the old Russian variety can get very hot particularly on the floor area in front of the front passenger's seat. I know of one tourist who had 30 films completely ruined by storing them against the front compartment in this location.

When film is in canisters, it is protected against high humidity but when used it is not. Humidity can also affect cameras so if you are a fanatic, use a humidity-proof case with rubber seals. This would prove invaluable for storing exposed film.

Ask permission before taking pictures of people; the Vietnamese are very friendly and rarely refuse. Travel light and make sure your camera has been serviced before the trip. Take lens tissue with you — it's difficult to get outside Ho Chi Minh. You will come across varied climatic conditions in Vietnam, generally in the southern provinces you can use slow film all the time but in Hue it's nearly always raining and remember the sky is usually grey in Tonkin.

Vietnamese Words and Phrases for Tourists
Vowel Sounds
a — as in bar (but shorter)
e — as in there
i — as in bin
y — as in be (but shorter)
o — as in saw (but shorter)
u — as in wheat

Consonant Sounds
ch — as in child
d — as in zip
g — as in dad
gi — as in zip
ng — as in singer
nh — as in onion
th — as in tip
tr — as in child
ch — as in eke

There are a variety of tones — too complex to be covered here.

Numbers

1 — *Mot*	11 — *Muoi mot*	100 — *Mot tram*
2 — *Hai*	12 — *Muoi hai*	1000 — *Mot ngan*
3 — *Ba*	13 — *Muoi ba*	
4 — *Bon*	14 — *Muoi bon*	
5 — *Nam*	15 — *Muoi lam*	
6 — *Sau*	16 — *Muoi sau*	
7 — *Bay*	17 — *Muoi bay*	
8 — *Tam*	18 — *Muoi tam*	
9 — *Chin*	19 — *Muoi chin*	
10 — *Muoi*	20 — *Hai muoi*	

Traditional greetings

These vary with whom the person is.

Hello — *Ong* — to and old man   *Tam biet* — Good bye

Anh — to a young man   *Cam on* — Thank you

Ba — to an old lady   *Hen gap lai* — See you again

Co — to a young lady   *Xin loi* — I am sorry

Chi — to an older lady   *Xin moi* — Please

Em — to younger people   *Bac co khoe khong* — How are you?

Chau — to a very young child   *Cam on binh thuong* — OK, thank you

Asking for Directions

O Dau — where

Ngan hang o dau? — where is the bank?

Buu dien — Post office

Benh vien — Hospital

Cho — market

Hieu sach — bookshop

Ngan hang — Bank

Ben xe tac xi — Taxi station

Khach san — hotel

Nha hang an — restaurant

Nha tho — Cathedral

Ho boi — Swimming pool

San bay — Airport

Ga xe lua — Train station

Ben xe — Bus station

Days of the Week

Thu hai — Monday

Thu ba —Tuesday

Thu tu — Wednesday

Thu nam — Thursday

Thu sau — Friday

Thu bay — Saturday

Thu nhat — Sunday

Months of the Year

Thang gieng — January

Thang hai — February

Thang ba — March

Thang tu — April

Thang nam — May

Thang sau — June

Thang bay — July

Thang tam — August

Thang chin — September

Thang muoi — October

Thang mot — November

Thang chap — December

Miscellaneous

Nha ve sinh o dau? — where is the toilet please?
Re ben trai (phai) — turn to the left (right)
Ten ong la gi? — what is your name?
Go I bac si den cho toi — Please send for a doctor
Toi bi rang tay — I have toothache
Toi bi di rua — I have diarrhoea

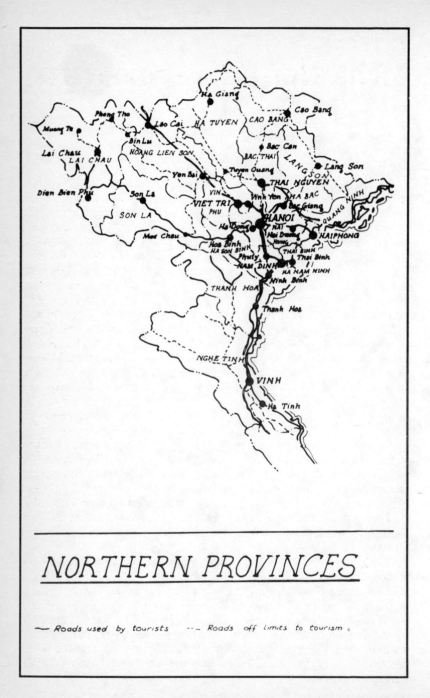

NORTHERN PROVINCES

— Roads used by tourists   --- Roads off limits to tourism

The Northern Provinces

HANOI

History

In the 3rd Century Hanoi only existed as a small village where the To Lich and Red rivers join. The area, aptly named "The Dragon's Navel" — Long Do, was established as a separate district called Tong Binh in 420. In the second half of the 10th Century the capital was transferred to Hoa Lu, now a favourite tourist centre near Ninh Binh in Ha Nam Ninh province. King Ly Cong Uan moved it to Thang-Long (where Hanoi is today) at the beginning of the Ly Dynasty 1010–1225. At this time the centre of the city was the sanctuary of King Ly who lived with his concubines in the area known as the Cam Thanh (Forbidden City). This formed the focal point of the Royal city surrounded on each side by the commoners' city. During the 216 years of the Ly Kings, Buddhism increased in importance and many Pagodas were built. The most famous Buddhist structures still remaining from this period are undoubtedly the One Pillar Pagoda, and the Tran Vu Temple, a must on any tourist itinerary of Hanoi. Even when the capital of old Vietnam was transferred to Thanh Hoa in 1400, Thang Long, then known as Dong Do, still retained its importance. Visitors to Hanoi will be told that in the 15th Century Le Thai To had a great victory against Ming invaders in Hanoi. There is a legend that after the victory he was sailing on lake Ho Guom (now known as "the lake of the restored sword") when a golden turtle snapped his sacred sword as he dipped it into the water. According to the legend the sacred sword, its mission fulfilled in the battle against the Ming, had been returned to Heaven.

Hanoi has never been a peaceful place. In the 15th Century the leader of the Tay Son rebellion, King Quang Trung, defeated a 200,000 strong Manchu army at Dong Do. During the Nguyen dynasty in 1802, the capital of Vietnam was transferred to Hue, but in 1831 it was transferred back to its present site at Hanoi. The city was attacked by the French in 1882 and although liberated in 1945, was attacked again in 1946. Final removal of French forces occurred after the battle of Dien Bien Phu in 1954. Hanoi was pounded by American bombs during the period April 17th 1966 to December 30th 1972. The worst

hit areas were undoubtedly the Kham Thien and An Duong districts
where visitors can still see some rebuilding activity.

Sightseeing

Most visitors to Hanoi are shown around the city by tourist guides.
Vietnamese Tourism is geared up for this, having guides for practically
every European language. There is no reason why you can't stroll
around by yourself but the authorities don't encourage it, don't let
them put you off, they are anyway taking less and less notice of it.
Most western visitors have pre-arranged itineraries and pre-booked
accommodation. Those arriving on business can easily hire an interpreter guide for the day if time is of the essence. Without an
interpreter, unless you speak Vietnamese, it is difficult to see all the
main sights in a few days' stay. For the adventurous, the best approach
is to get an elaborate map of the city from the Foreign Language
Bookshop, 61 Trang Tien Street, or the State Bookshop, 40 Trang
Tien Street. The next question is how do you get there? Any visitor to
Hanoi will easily find the Ho Chi Minh mausoleum in Quan Ba Dinh
(Ba Dinh Sqaure) — it's around the corner from the One Pillar
Pagoda. Walk from here down Dien Bien Phu Boulevard and after
about 10 minutes, you will arrive at Trang Thi Avenue. If you walk
along this for another 10 minutes you will pass the southern part of the
Lake of the Restored Sword. You can't miss Trang Tien Street if you
continue directly to the end of Trang Thi Avenue. A warning however
— when you get to the bookshops there is no guarantee that you will
be able to purchase a map of Hanoi — they are frequently sold out.
Try the souvenir shop in the Thang Loi Tourist hotel.

However you tour the city you will be rewarded by the friendliness
of the people and the charming nature of the surroundings. Many
visitors to Hanoi expect to see a considerable amount of devastation —
they are in for a surprise. There is little evidence of war damage. There
is no hostility towards westerners, even Americans are only eyed with
amiable curiosity.

Hanoi is a delightful city which comes alive in the rush hours.
Thousands of bicycles transporting conical hats mingle with jeeps and
trucks and the occasional water buffalo. The cream-coloured houses,
slightly discoloured with age, tell the visitor that Hanoi has seen better
times. Much of the architecture is decidedly French and the street
names remind the historian of past events, famous insurrectionists,
generals and kings.

At the junction of Trang Tien and Nam Bo is the largest store in
Hanoi. Inside, the shelves are very bare and queues are reminiscent of
Russian cities.

An excellent itinerary, if one wants to see the real Hanoi, is to head
north from Trang Tien Street around Ho Hoan Kiem — the Lake of

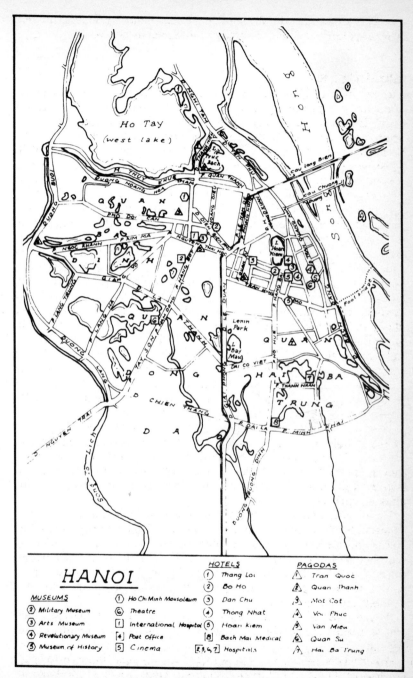

HANOI

MUSEUMS
② Military Museum
③ Arts Museum
④ Revolutionary Museum
⑤ Museum of History

① Ho Chi Minh Mausoleum
⑥ Theatre
Ⅰ International Hospital
④ Post Office
⑤ Cinema

HOTELS
① Thang Loi
② Bo Ho
③ Dan Chu
④ Thong Nhat
⑤ Hoan kiem
⑧ Bach Mai Medical
Ⅰ,3,6,7 Hospitals

PAGODAS
△₁ Tran Quoc
△₂ Quan Thanh
△₃ Mot Cot
△₄ Voi Phuc
△₅ Van Mieu
△₆ Quan Su
△₇ Hai Ba Trung

the Restored Sword. You will pass the Tortoise Tower and a statue to the Golden Tortoise (Turtle). At the furthest point on the lake, after passing the Ngoc Son Temple, if you continue in a straight line along Dinh Tien Hoang Street, you will enter the "old quarter" of Hanoi. This is known as Dong Kinh Nghia Thuc, named after a great revolutionary cultural movement led by Luong Van Can. The old quarter is a labyrinth of tiny sreets which sell everything from spoons made out of recycled B–52 bombers, to herbal medicines used as a cure for snake bites. The streets in the area are named after the produce they sell. From Silk Street, where there are masses of embroidery shops, one can hop onto a tram for a few minutes which will take you to Dong Xuan market. The flower market along Hang Luoc Street is an amazing spectacle, especially just before Tet — the New Year's festival. It is interesting to zig-zag your way through the tiny streets with evocative names such as Paper Street, Cotton Street, Jeweller's Street, Medicine Stret, Fish Street, Basket Street and Cantonese Street. Tourists can pick up excellent bargains – leather-work, mother of pearl inlays, hats, tinware, baskets, badges and silkware. The Vietnamese are excellent bargainers and most goods can be bought for half the asking price. In the old quarter is the famous Hang Ngang Street where, in 1945, Ho Chi Minh wrote the Declaration of Independence.

Easily the best way to see Hanoi is to hire a bicycle. The reception at the tourist hotels will advise you how to do this. The Tourist Authority prefer to send a guide with you but there is no reason why you can't explore by yourself. It is not advisable during the rush hours unless you have thoroughly tested out the route beforehand. The authorities are becoming more used to seeing westerners on bicyles although it is still a fairly rare sight. They still prefer you to have a chaperone.

A pagoda tour by bicycle

You will need a good map of Hanoi and it is very useful but not essential to take a friend who speaks Vietnamese. Since most for-eigners stay at the Thang Loi Hotel, the tour starts from here. You first head down Duong Nghi Tam after turning right out of the Thang Loi Hotel. At the first junction with four roads, turn right (at right angles) down Duong Thanh Nien. On the right is the West Lake (Ho Tay). The Vietnamese will tell you about the legend of the fox spirit with nine tails which lived in this area before the lake appeared. A rather far-fetched story is told to Vietnamese school children about the origins of the lake. A vast bronze bell was made by a Buddhist monk, Khong Lo, whose sound carried so far that it reached a golden buffalo calf. The calf thought that the sound was his mother calling and rushed to the area. It stamped on the ground so hard that a lake appeared under its hoofs. On the left-hand side of the road is Truc Bach lake where a magnificent Summer Palace was once built by a Trinh lord.

Continuing down Duong Thanh Nien you reach **The Tran Quoc Pogoda**. This is not at all spectacular. The only thing of interest is the Stelae (1639) which carries an inscription on the history of the pagoda.

Continuing down towards Ho Chi Minh's mausoleum along Duong Thanh Nien you come to the very ornate Quan Thanh Pagoda which is well worth a visit. The temple is dedicated to Tran Vo and was built during the Ly dynasty (1010–1225). The huge bronze bell which it houses was cast in 1677. There is also a magnificent bronze statue.

Next on the itinerary is the **One Pillar Pagoda (Chua Mot Cot)**. This is reached by heading straight down Duong Hung Vuong and turning right at Chua Mot Cot road. The best time for a photographer to visit this is about 5pm when the small wooden frame pagoda glows in the setting sun. Originally it was built in 1049 and restored in 1105. Its form evokes a lotus. King Ly Thai To, who had no son, dreamed that the Goddess Quan Am, seated on a lotus flower, handed him a male child. He married a peasant girl and they were blessed with a son. In token of gratitude he had the pagoda built and dedicated it to the Goddess Bodhisatva. Occasionally, a visitor may be lucky enough to come across a pilgrim paying homage to Quan Am at the One Pillar Pagoda shrine.

The **Quan Su Pagoda** is reached by cycling to the end of Dien Bien Phu Boulevard which is reached from the One Pillar Pagoda by continuing to the end of Chua Mot Cot road. The second right turning is taken off Trang Thi road down Pho Quan Su which leads to Quan Su Pagoda. This is a rewarding visit best made on Sunday morning when there is Buddhist ceremony. The outside is very Chinese looking, and inside is a magnificent central altar with figures of Sakya at birth, Sayka Mouni — Buddha of the Present, Di Da — Buddha of the Past, and Di Lac — Buddha of the future. Also represented is Quan Am, the Goddess Bodhisatva and her attendants.

Next, retrace your route back to the beginning of Dien Bien Phu and turn left down Duong Nam Bo past Lenin Park and lake Ho Bay Mau and turn left down Dai Co Viet. Continue straight until Tran Khat Chan and take the second turning on the left which leads to **Hai Ba Trung** (occasionally weapon training can be seen in Lenin park). Here you will see a statue of the two Trung sisters kneeling with their arms raised. This was first built in 1142.

This pagoda is a little out of the way and should be omitted if time is of the essence.

Next on the itinerary is **Van Mieu — The Temple of Literature**. Retrace the steps back to Dien Bien Phu Boulevard and cycle down Pho Nguyen Thai Hoc. The fifth turning on the left leads to the Temple of Literature. This deserves a special mention and should definitely be visited. It became the first centre of higher education for

The One Pillar Pagoda in Hanoi.

Quoc Tu Giam or the National Academy. The Temple, which is dedicated to Confucius, was founded in 1070 during the reign of Ly Thanh Tong. Vietnamese scholars had great respect for Confucius, an eminent Chinese master philosopher. The Temple, which is visited by pilgrims from all parts of the country, has become a museum piece. For a long time the Temple of Literature was the symbol of an intellectual life carefully fostered in feudal Vietnam. A central path extends from the main gate, and the whole complex is divided longitudinally into five parts by walls and gates.

The grounds are entered via the Van Mieu Gate, the main gate of the Temple. A path through a well-kept garden leads to the Dai Trung gate and from here pavements extend to the Khue Van Cac known as the Mirador of the Khue Constellation. This gate is topped by a wooden pavilion endowed with a two-storey roof with four windows shaped like the sun, with rays which open onto the four cardinal points.

The stelae bear the names of the laureates of royal examinations held over a period of three hundred years (1484–1787).

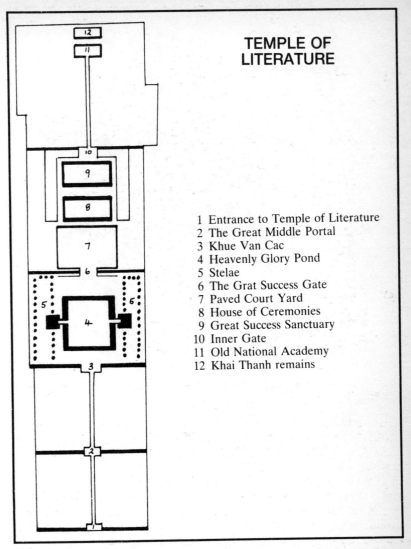

TEMPLE OF LITERATURE

1 Entrance to Temple of Literature
2 The Great Middle Portal
3 Khue Van Cac
4 Heavenly Glory Pond
5 Stelae
6 The Grat Success Gate
7 Paved Court Yard
8 House of Ceremonies
9 Great Success Sanctuary
10 Inner Gate
11 Old National Academy
12 Khai Thanh remains

You enter the fourth part which is the temple proper via the Great Success Gate (Dai Thanh). The House of Ceremonies dedicated to Confucius and his disciples is directly opposite. The great bronze bell cast in 1768 is kept here. In the Bai Duong or House of Ceremonies, sacrifices were offered in honour of Confucius. Behind it is the Great Success Sanctuary, and the the eastern gate. The fifth and last part is situated along Nguyen Thai Hoc Street — the remains of the sanctuary of the saints dedicated to the parents of Confucius.

Stelae Temple of Literature, Hanoi.

If you wish, you can retrace your steps and visit Ba Dinh Square to see Ho Chi Minh's Mausoleum. This is known to the Vietnamese as Lang Bac. It was inaugurated on September 2nd 1975. The lotus-like architecture is a reminder of Lang Sen, Lotus Village, where he came from in Nghe Tinh province. The embalmed body of the President lies on top of a three-tiered platform inside a cold roon.

Warning: Photographers are not allowed beyond a point stipulated by the guards in Ba Dinh Square. They are very strict indeed. No photography is allowed inside the mausoleum.

Museums
The history museum

This is on Trang Tien Street a little way down from the bookshops and main department store. It was built in 1895 during French times. At one time it was a history and archaeological research institute with a museum attached (Ecole Française d'Extrême-Orient). It became the History Museum of Vietnam in 1958. Being an important cultural and scientific research centre it has professional contact with 85 cultural centres and museums in the world.

The history of Vietnam is extremely complicated and those interested should spend many happy hours here. Take an interpreter along — it's essential. During the heavy bombing raids in Hanoi the major exhibits were not damaged because they had been transported elsewhere. The museum is arranged so that each room relates to a particular dynasty. You will often run into crowds of schoolchildren since the Vietnamese are very keen on their children having extensive knowledge of their history. The section on prehistoric man dating back to the middle Pliocene (500,000 years ago) is very informative. There are exhibits of primitive tools made from horn, bamboo, coconut shells and bone. Discoveries from Neolithic sites (4000 BC) indicate that rice was grown in Vietnam at this time. The museum even contains Neolithic graves of about 3000 BC. Many bronze age implements are displayed, discovered around Than Hoa. The bronze drum from Ngoc Lu in Ha Nam Ninh province is a masterpiece showing carvings of deer, birds, horses, boats and warriors. There is also a magnificent rice urn.

There is the story of the Hong Bang Family — 2879 BC–258 BC (2,622 years) when the name of the country was Van Lang and the capital was Vinh Phu. During the Au Lac period when this was the name given to Vietnam the Thuc family ruled (257 BC–208 BC). Co Loa citadel, which can be visited about 20km from Hanoi, has been excavated. There is a model of this citadel in the museum.

The various uprisings that occurred against the Chinese occupation from 111 BC are celebrated by exhibits about the Trung sisters (40–43 AD), Dame Trieu (248 AD), Mai Thuc Loan (722) and Khuc Thua Du (905). An account of the battle of the Bach Dang River against the Mongols is displayed here as well as in the revolutionary museum.

Tourists who have Ninh Binh on their programmes will be interested in the exhibits about the Dinh dynasty (968–980) and the Le dynasty (980–1009) because they will see the temples dedicated to King Dinh Bo Linh and General Le at Hoa-Lu, the ancient capital of Vietnam. There is a model of this old capital at the museum and a portrait of Le Dai Hang (General Le).

There is a magnificent Buddhist statue from the first Ly dynasty (1010–1225) when the country was called Dai Viet and its capital was

Thang Long. During this period the influence of Buddhism spread widely.

The feudal social structure of the Tran dynasty (1407–1413) is depicted in an elaborate painting. There are models of the battles against Mongol invaders during the period. There is a large ornate tortoise sculpture on the gravestone of Le Loi to commemorate the 'Lake of the Restored Sword' story. The remarkable sculpture of the woman Buddha with a thousand eyes and thousand hands makes a somewhat creepy sight.

The exhibits from the second Le dynasty (1533–1788) tell the story of the trouble between the Nguyen families in the South and the Trinh in the North. The Tay Son room tells the story of the famous Tay Son rebellion which began in Binh Dinh near Quynhon in 1771. Many primitive weapons used during this period are exhibited (the story of the Tay Son rebellion is included under Quynhon section in this book).

The room set aside for exhibits from the Nguyen dynasty (1802–1945) will be of considerable interest to tourists going to Hue, the old Imperial capital of Vietnam. There is a throne and many costumes and artefacts of 13 Nguyen kings.

The arts museum — Nguyen Thai Hoc (Tel: 52830)
A visit here can be combined with the Van Mieu temple because it is next to it. It was opened in the mid-sixties when the Americans started bombing North Vietnam. There is a display of ancient culture including bronze drums, bronze statues and stone-made ornaments. Many similarities will be seen with Chinese art. Like Chinese sculpture, Vietnamese sculpture centres readily on the statues in pagodas and in the objects of private or public workshop. Visitors to the museum will also notice the influence of Cham art on Vietnamese art particularly from exhibits from Phat-Tich pagoda, which were obviously designed by the Cham people. The Vietnamese paintings exhibited are often remarkable for their naïve simplicity. There are many works depicting Tet — the New Year festival, religious scenes, fine landscapes and portraits.

The revolutionary museum — 25 Tong Dan Street.
Founded in 1959 the museum is near the History Museum. It covers the struggles of the Vietnamese people in a series of displays in 10 rooms.

Room 1 What stands out is the huge bronze war drum dating back to 2400 BC. Visitors wonder what the long sticks are. If they have been to Halong Bay they will have been told about the battle of the Bach Dang river where a Mongol fleet was crippled with wooden stakes driven hard into the river beds. You will need an interpreter to read the letters of Nguyen Trai, a well known Vietnamese academic. The novels and poems of the very famous Nguyen Du are on display.

Room 2 What takes your eye are the hideous frames used to lock people up during the Yen The peasant war. The struggles of Phan Dinh Phung involved in this war are depicted. The resistance to French occupation is really brought to light when one sees the portraits of martyrs who sacrificed themselves for the independence of Vietnam.

Room 3 This is dedicated to the various stages of the life of President Ho Chi Minh. It even has a picture of the small room in Paris where he worked as a photographer's assistant. It tells the story of his exploits in France, England, Russia and China. The book written by Ho Chi Minh in French, *Le Proces de la Colonisation Française*, is on display. There are details on the formation of the Vietnam Communist Party in Hong Kong which Ho instigated. A picture is displayed of the British lawyer who succeeded in bringing about his release from jail in Hong Kong. There are also photographs of a communist meeting in Moscow in 1933 which Ho attended while studying at the Lenin Institute, the anti-fascist demonstrations in Hanoi in 1936, and a cave in which he lived during Japanese occupation of Vietnam. Ho Chi Minh was greatly loved by his people. Proudly displayed are his suitcase, dishes, suit, poems and the engravings of Marx on the cave wall. There is the story of the formation of the 'Vietnam Independence League', and a copy of Ho's *History of Vietnam* written in 1942. Rather upsetting are the pictures of emaciated bodies from the famine of 1944–45.

Room 4 A variety of insurrections are depicted here. These include the invasion of Vietnam by Chinese and Gurkhas and, of course, the French. A model depicting the attack on the French Governor's Palace in 1945 is shown, and even the microphone through which Uncle Ho read the Declaration of Independence on September 2nd 1945 from Ba Dinh Square. Photographs of the fighting against the Japanese are on show, and a rather gruesome collection of weapons stolen from the French. The battle of Dien Bien Phu is well represented by a model, a picture of the French surrender, and the messages of condolence from Eisenhower and Churchill to General Castries. As you pass out of this hall, a massive French-style guillotine catches your eye.

Rooms 5, 6 and 7 These depict the struggle against the United States.

Room 5 Contains photographic displays of weapons used by the French and supplied by the US. There is a picture of Richard Nixon's visit to Vietnam and of Ngo Dinh Diem's torturing of captives. The Kennedy era, 1960–1964, is well documented.

Room 6 This contains the very famous picture of the first landing of US Marines in Danang on March 6th 1965 during Johnson's presidency, and disturbing scenes of violent destruction.

Room 7　If you are easily upset, I would avoid this room because it depicts US troops carrying severed heads, and public executions. The rest of the display featuring photographs of captured US pilots and the 1972 December bombings of Hanoi are truly devastating. There are pictures of the last troops leaving Vietnam on March 15th 1973. As you leave this hall you pass the torture box, only about 8 feet square and 4 feet high. in which up to 20 or 50 prisoners were dumped. These were often placed in the sun and sometimes shot at.

Room 8　Features booby-traps used by resistance fighters against their enemies. The execution photographs by Nguyen Van Troi, who made an attempt on the life of Robert McNamara, are prominently displayed.

Room 9　Contains scenes of the 1973–1975 war in South Vietnam together with pictures of the liberation of Saigon on April 30th 1975.

Room 10　Contains exhibitions of objects which are anti-Vietnam war. This includes baskets with anti-war slogans and even belts and buttons with the same messages.

The army museum — Dien Bien Phu Street, Tel: 58101
This is overlooked by the Flag-Tower. It has over 3,000 exhibits on the Vietnamese People's Armed Forces. Explicit displays include the Dien Bien Phu campaign ending in 1954, and the Ho Chi Minh campaign against the US, ending in 1975.

No 48 Hang Ngang Street
This is in the old part of Hanoi and is a dwelling house turned into a museum. Here, in 1945, President Ho Chi Minh wrote the famous Declaration of Independence.

The Ho Chi Minh museum
This is under construction in Hanoi. It is going to be a lotus-shaped polygonal structure located in President Ho Chi Minh's memorial compound which includes his mausoleum, the Presidential Palace and his house and garden. The exterior walls will be tiled with marble and a door will be set in each of the four flat corners. It is intended to evoke a white lotus enclosing a red marble block (the stamens) which symbolises President Ho Chi Minh's spirit. The museum is expected to be completed on May 19th 1989 in preparation for the celebration of President Ho Chi Minh's birth centenary (May 19th 1890 — May 19th 1990).

Tourist Facilities — Hanoi
Hotels
The main hotels used by the Tourist Authority in Hanoi are the Thang Loi and the Thong Nhat.

Thang Loi (H1 on map) Yen Phu Street, Hanoi. Tel: 58211.

This is a large hotel newly built on the outskirts of Hanoi. It is about the standard of a second class hotel in Bangkok. Rooms are available for about 400 people. Special rooms are available for VIPs such as diplomats. The price is around US$ 50 for a first class room/night.

Services: Laundry, telex, telegram service, souvenir shop, bar, two restaurants, swimming pool, dance every Saturday night. For those who like peace and quiet, this is not the place to stay on a Saturday night when all the youth of Hanoi seem to be there.

The Hotel is nicely situated on the edge of Ho Tay (west lake). The service is a bit impersonal because of its size. The food is satisfactory but nothing special. Do not be alarmed if you see the occasional rat running through the restaurants, there are rats everywhere in Hanoi. Make sure you don't leave your lights on in your room at night with the windows open — your walls will be black with insects.

Thong Nhat (H5 on map) 15 Ngo Quyen Street, Hanoi. Tel: 52785 — 58221.

This is well situated in the centre of Hanoi near the Ho Koan Kiem (the Lake of Restored Sword). It has the same facilities as the Thang Loi but is a little run down. In Bangkok it would be rated as a third class hotel. There are 192 rooms. Some of the mosquito nets have holes. Eight special rooms are around US$ 50, 1st class at around US$ 37 single, US$ 42 double, 2nd class, US$ 33 single, US$ 36 double, 3rd class US$ 26 single, US$ 29 double. This hotel is being improved all the time. Those requesting the Thong Nhat to the Tourist Authority are often put in the Thang Loi. A lot of journalists stay in the Thong Nhat.

There is a dance, 1960s style, at the Thong Nhat every Saturday night from 8.00 to 10.00. Around the corner is the Bao Chi Club which is reserved for journalists — it's easy to get in even if you aren't a journalist. If you want to mix with a western crowd, go to the Australian Embassy's Billabong Club. First get an invitation from a diplomat staying at the Thang Loi hotel — there are always plenty there and you can spot them a mile off.

Smaller hotels are available in Hanoi but are generally only used by the Tourist Authority when the others are full up, for instance at Tet. Examples of these are:

Bo Ho Hotel (map reference H2) 1 Ba Trieu. Tel: 52075.
Dan Chu Hotel (map reference H3) 2 Nguyen Khac Can. Tel: 53323 — 54344 — 54937.
Hoan Kiem Hotel (map reference H4) 25 Tran Hung Do. Tel: 56547.

All these have simple facilities, restaurant, bar, laundry service, and are situated in the centre of the city. The average price is US$ 25 for single, US$30 double. It is quite possible that if you request one of these hotels with the Tourist Authority, you will be put into better class accommodation. The Authorities will give no reason for this. They are very comfortable Vietnamese style hotels.

Restaurants

These are found in the main tourist hotels. There are many street restaurants scattered throughout the city. The best places to eat are in the old part of Hanoi. The restaurant stools are very uncomfortable: they were built for midgets!

Some useful phrases for use in a street restaurant
May I have the bill please? — *Xin tinh tien?*
I want something to eat (to drink) — *Toi muon an (Uong)*
Could I have some coffee please? — *Dong chi bac lam on cho toi ca phe?*
I like chicken — *Toi thich an thit ga*
I don't like fish — *Toi khong thich an ca*
I'm thirsty — *Toi khat*
May I have the menu please? — *Cho toi xin thuc don?*
How much — *Bao nhieu tien*
May I have? — *Cho toi xin?*
Orange juice — *Nuoc cam*
Soft drink — *Nuoc ngot*
Beer — *Bia*
Banana — *Chuoi*
Papaya — *Du du*
Pineapple — *Dua*
Tea — *Nuoc tra*
Boiled water — *Nuoc soi*
Pepper — *Hat tieu*
Salt — *Muoi*
Fish sauce — *Nuoc mam*
Soy sauce — *Xi dau*

Typical delicacies found in the old quarter in Hanoi
Pho — Excellent for breakfast, dinner or tea. This is one of the most popular dishes in Hanoi. It is a soup made from cooked rice noodles with shredded beef or chicken and seasonings (shallot, parsley) on top. It has a broth stock made from shin bones, prawns, ginger root and fish sauce. Lemon and chilli are often added to make it more tasty.
Mien luon — A form of small eel soup with mushrooms, onions, and chicken, Vermicelli is added.
Cha — This fried pork dish is best done over charcoal.
Banh cuon — A minced filling is put into pancakes which are steamed. A delicious sauce is available with this made from peppers, cloves, garlic, salt, sweeteners and vinegar.
Gio — Rolled up pork shredded and cooked in banana leaves.

Nem — In Hanoi, a filling of crab, vermicelli, onions, eggs and mushrooms is fried inside a thin rice pancake. If you want this in the southern provinces of Vietnam ask for *cha gio*.

Ech tam bot ran — This is frog meat soaked in batter served with a vinegar and pepper fish sauce.

Oc nhoi (snail) — Chopped snail meat is put into ginger leaves with a variety of fillings and cooked.

If you fancy a dessert, try some of these:

Mut — A form of sweetened candied fruit made from lotus seeds, kumquat, coconut or ginger.

Banh com — Doesn't appeal to many westerners but worth trying. It's a cake with a filling of mung bean paste.

Com — Young sticky rice.

Banh dau xanh — This melts when it is put on the tongue — it's made of mung beans and sticky rice cake.

Vietnamese food is delicious — they will not thank you if you compare it to Chinese food!

Other addresses and telephone numbers

First Aid — Tel: 05.

Fire Brigade — Tel: 08.

Police — Tel: 03.

Post Office — The Central Post Office, Dinh Tien Hoang Street. Tel: 57036.

The International Post Office, 75 Dinh Tien Hoang Street. Tel: 54413.

Major International Bank — 7 Le Lai. Tel: 54169

Tourist Souvenir Shop — 30A Ly Thuong Kiet.

This stocks some very high class souvenirs especially lacquerware and ceramics.

Hospitals

Major International Hospital — Benh Vien Quoc Te, Kim Lien Street, Hanoi. Tel: 43728.

This is where tourists can be taken in an emergency.

Viet-Xo Hospital 1 Tran Khanh Du. Tel: 52231.

Viet-Duc Hospital 40 Trang Thi. Tel: 53531.

Xanh Pon Hospital 59 Tran Phu. Tel: 55191.

Benh Vien Bach Mai Nga Tu Vong Street, Hanoi. Tel: 54385.

This is a very famous hospital in Hanoi, which was extensively damaged during the US bombing raids.

Theatres

Central Theatre Duong Trang Tien.

Workers Cultural House Duong Tran Hung Dao.

The Circus
It is in Lenin Park, and I can recommend it strongly. It's up to the standard of a good Russian circus. Tickets for this are booked through the Tourist Office, 18 Ly Thuong Kiet, Tel: 54290. A visit can be arranged through the reception at the Thang Loi Hotel. Tourists are given VIP treatment — ringside seats with cushions! I don't see any reason why tourists can't just go along, but I'm told it's not done like this — the reason given is that it is often heavily booked!

Bookshops
Foreign Language Bookshop, 61 Trang Tien Street. Tel: 57043.
Thong Nhat Bookshop, 17 Ngo Quyen Street. Tel: 57351.
The State Bookshop, 40 Trang Tien Street. Tel: 54282.

Shops
General Department Store, Trang Tien Street. Tel: 53042.
The Department Store, 5 Nam Bo Street. Tel: 55814.
The International Shop, Le Thai To Street. Tel: 55517.
The Fine Arts Shop, 25 Hang Khay Street. Tel: 55845.

Library
The National Library, 31 Trang Thi Street. Tel: 52643.
The Foreign Languages Publishing House, 46 Tran Hung Dao Street. Tel: 53841.

Cinemas
Very occasionally American films with Vietnamese sub-titles are shown. Films are often in Russian.
Bac Do Cinema, 39 Hang Giay. Tel: 55611.
Cong Nhan Cinema, 42 Trang Tien. Tel: 57252.
Hong Ha Cinema, 51 Duong Thanh. Tel: 52803.

The Outskirts of Hanoi

Da Tong Pagoda
This is well worth a visit particularly for photographers. It contains a statue of the Goddess of Mercy (Avalokitecvara) with one thousand eyes and one thousand hands. This was made using the ancient technique of Vietnamese sculpture in which bamboo strips are used to make statues. The numerous eyes and hands express the popular belief that the Goddess knows a lot about human misfortunes and can do a lot to relieve them. A number of the arms and hands are made of woven bamboo strips coated with gold and vermilion lacquer.

Dame Magnolia Temple
This is in her native village Sui, Gia Lam district on the outskirts of the city.
   When she was a girl she was called Le Thi Menh. It was her husband, King Ly Thang Tong (1054–1072), who called her Dame

Magnolia because he had seen her first under a magnolia tree when he was on the way to a pagoda to pray for a son. She bore him a son who became King Ly Nhan Tong. A devout Buddhist, she left a study which shed light on the history of Buddhism in Vietnam. Over 100 pagodas and towers were built with her encouragement including the famous Chuong Son tower in Ha Nam Ninh.

Outside Hanoi

The Den Citadel
This is in Cu An hamlet in Me Linh district 40 km from Hanoi. It is dedicated to the Trung sisters, Trung Trac and her younger sister Trung Nhi. These two national heroines defeated the Chinese occupation troops under the command of Su Ting in AD 40. The vestiges of a temple for the worship of Trung Nhi are seen on a hill on the southern part of the citadel. The locals call it the citadel with three ponds.

Today it is an unspectacular place but worth visiting if you are a devotee of Vietnamese history.

Tien La Temple
At Tien La in Thai Binh province, you would only visit this temple if you had a lot of spare time. It is dedicated to Bat Nan one of the women warriors who assisted the Trung sisters in the battle against the eastern Han. There is a statute of Bat Nan inside the temple. She was born in Phuong Lau in Vinh Phu province and became an expert in martial arts before joining the Trung sisters' campaign.

The Chua Thay Pagoda
This is 60 km from Hanoi in Sai Son village, Quoc Oai district, Ha Son Binh province. It was built during the Ly dynasty (11th Century). Inside is a statue of Tu Dao Hanh. Before he lived in this pagoda, he had been a medical man in his native village. He was buried in a cave near the pagoda site. According to an ancient legend, King Ly Than Tong and his wife Sung Hien Hau came to this pagoda and prayed for a son. It is believed that Tu Dao Hanh, the late monk of the pagoda, was reincarnated as their son.

The pagoda is well worth a visit. There are a variety of enclosures containing Buddhist figures. The inner enclosure of Chua Thay has well preserved statues of Buddhas of the past, present and future. A statue of Tu Dao Hanh in a yellow robe is seated behind the statue of Sakya at brith.

In the second enclosure there are remarkable statues of good and bad guardians and Tuyet Son, a monk depicted with a pink face.

Eight kilometres further on is the Tay Phong pagoda, very similar to the one inside but very ornate from the outside. The handicraft shop in Hang Khay street, Hanoi, sells statues which are modelled on those in

Tay Phong. They are beautifully carved by the fine arts company in Longan.

Agricultural cooperatives

A visit can be organised through Vietnam Tourist Authority to the Da Ton agricultural cooperative on the outskirts of Hanoi. This is run by Le Van Bui, chairman of the cooperative. Visitors will be given a traditional cup of tea while he tells them about the cooperative's accomplishments. On the walls are red and yellow banners, 'Certificates of Achievement'.

The cooperative is run by a committee with Le Van Bui in charge. Members of the committee are recruited from the most educated, who are expected to behave in a manner befitting their status. The whole community works as a unit, not as individuals. The goods produced are sold in government-run shops and the proceeds are used to buy new tools, tractors, other machinery, fertiliser and pesticides. The peasants are paid a fixed sum for eight hours work a day (five days a week).

In Da Ton, since it is such a thriving concern, each worker has been given 0.05 acres where they can keep their own pigs, chickens, pigeons and grow crops. The produce from this belongs to the household.

The workers are justly very proud of its achievements. From a 100 hectare garden they produce two tons of fruit a season (oranges, tangerines and guava). They grow soya, groundnut and maize, farm fish ponds raising small fry to sell to other cooperatives, and breed pigs. The workers are skilled in animal husbandry and have excellent crop rotation schemes.

Alternative cooperatives

Vietnam Tourism also run trips to the Yen So cooperative on the outskirts of Hanoi. This is very similar but also has carpet making facilities. Another interest is Gia Tan cooperative, 40 miles east of Hanoi in Hai Hung province. In addition to the normal production scheme, they also have a brick making establishment, embroidery, animal food processing, and water conservation projects.

Visit to a carpet enterprise

Some tourists may wish to buy woollen carpets. It is no problem to take these out of the country. They are woven by hand and are absolutely unique.

The Dong Da enterprise in Hanoi is the place to visit. It has close relations with the College of Industrial Arts and the Fine Arts College in Hanoi. Woollen carpets are only made in Vietnam in Hanoi, Hai Phong and Ha Bac.

The director of the enterprise, Ngo Quang Tu, will show you around. The workers are exceptionally skilful, designs being produced for them by professional artists. Some are so intricate that they are more like tapestries than carpets.

Expect to pay $100 for a medium size rug.

Hanoi's college of industrial arts

Very few visitors go here but it is well worth requesting for its ceramics department. Vietnamese ceramics are symmetrically perfect and often have a peacock motif. Many are copies of relics from the Ly and Tran dynasties (11th–14th Century).

You will be shown the various stages in ceramic manufacture, moulding the clay, shaping, sculpturing, baking, painting and varnishing. Many vase designs come from the Dong Thanh Cooperative in Quang Ninh Ceramic Enterprise.

Tourists can feast their eyes upon pots and vases with designs featuring peach trees, pear trees, chrysanthemums, cacti, pheasants, peacocks, etc. The enamels are varied, jade coloured, ivory or blue.

The exhibits are for sale ranging in price from US$1 to over $100.

Ba Trang ceramics village

This is easily combined with the visit to the College of Industrial Arts. The village has long been known throughout Vietnam for its highly original ceramic products. It has over 800 kilns in operation and turns out over a million products per year. The village is keen on training young craftsmen and creating new designs to satisfy varied tastes. It has made a special study of glazes made during the 10th to 13th Centuries.

Well known in the village are the Nguyen Duc Duong family who make 14 kinds of household and ornamental articles. Their 11 year old son, Nguyen Duc Huy, is already a master craftsman. He has won a major competition sponsored by the Thieu Nien Tien Phong.

The Gia Lam sewing enterprise for dislabled soldiers

A visit here may be distressing for some people. It was set up twelve years ago in Hanoi's suburban district of Gia Lam.

The director, Luu Dinh Nghi, informs visitors that the soldiers attend job training courses before working at the Enterprise. Besides wages, the disabled soldiers receive indemnities for their injuries and social welfare.

It now has 825 members, half of which are wounded soldiers. They produce 1–1.2 million products every year. These include clothes for daily life and high quality garments made to measure.

Visit to an invalid camp

Western tourists are often surprised that Vietnam Tourism will organise a visit to a camp for badly injured soldiers. There are 16 of these in North Vietnam.

Not many tourists wish to visit, but those who do will be in for a warm welcome. It is possible to request to visit Camp Number 1 in Thuan Thanh district of Ha Bac province. This is an interesting journey taking about one and a half hours by car from Hanoi. Anybody who is easily upset should definitely stay away because many of the inmates have lost limbs and are paralysed. They have workshops for making transistor radios and other electrical goods, gardens, and crèches for the children of invalid families.

They love to get foreign visitors and a few presents would be greatly appreciated.

VISIT TO MINORITY PEOPLES AND TO DIEN BIEN PHU

If you request this trip between May and October you will probably be turned down. Between 300–400 mm of rain falls per month during this period. The road is fine as far as Son La but afterwards, due to the monsoons, it is often washed away or a mountain slides over it! The best months recommended for travel are January and February. I have heard that tourists have successfully completed the trip in November and December when the rainfall is only slightly higher. If you come to Vietnam only to visit Dien Bien Phu be warned that the Tourist Authority cancels the trip at very short notice (due to the road conditions) and that you will then be offered an alternative programme.

Consult programme 6 in the Appendix to see what is involved. Those interested in seeing minority people should arrange for an extension to this tour before arriving in Vietnam. A suitable new programme would require at least four or five more days. Hoa Binh could be extended to see the two villages of the Muong people. The guide at the Hoa Binh guest house is Muong and he will escort you. Be warned, however, that the Muong are often visited by westerners because programmes 4, 5 and 15 also visit the area. They are extremely camera shy and will probably disappear at the first sight of a westerner. Your Muong guide will arrange a musical performance in the evening providing you request it in plenty of time. It is best to request it in Hanoi before leaving for Hoa Binh. Your guide will give you facts about the Muong people over a cup of tea at the guest house. The accommodation here is very basic with plenty of holes for mosquitoes to get in and the noise from wood-boring beetles can be rather bad at night!

The Muong people

The Muong children are taught verbally — they have no written language. They are sometimes called the Mol Mual and the Muan. The

300,000 or so who live in the Ha Son Binh province rear pigs and poultry, and hunt with crossbows. Their buffalo herds can be heard from long distances away because of the tinkling of their bells. They know their forests well and collect cardamom, honey, bamboo, fungi and many medicinal herbs.

They grow rice by the slash and burn method. During the fight against French occupation they fought alongside the Viet and formed guerrilla groups. Their attack on Hoa Binh town in January 1891 is well known. Their villages are called *quel* or *quen* and their stilted houses are of a similar design to the Black Thai. The master of a group of *quel* is called *lang cun*. it is his job to administrate and generally keep an eye out for trouble. It is still traditional that the entire population of a hamlet look after one field of the headman. The system where the *lang cun* rules is now only seen in very isolated groups and the Muong villages visited by tourists will work together on a cooperative basis.

Extension to see White Thai Minority
The main area of the white Thai villages is in the Mai Chau region of Son La province. This is off the normal route to Dien Bien Phu. Mai Chau lies in a deep valley about 60 km from Hoa Binh. The best time to visit is in the late afternoon when the setting sun produces a yellow glow. Gold panning has been practised in the area for well over a century. The gold dust is separated with mercury which can later be evaporated to yield the gold. The people can earn about three times as much as a city dweller extracting gold from the streams. Very few tourists visit the area so the people are not too shy of westerners. The white Thai minority have developed very effective irrigation systems and grow abundant supplies of rice. Very few now wear the traditional costume. Their tortoise-shell shaped houses produce some very interesting landscapes for the photographer. Their villages, called *ban*, often have as many as 50 houses. The Thai, unlike the Muong, can write and many famous poets have grown up in the area. It is said that illiteracy among them is a thing of the past. Many have graduated from university to become engineers, doctors, teachers, writers and even actors. Some have become members of the national assembly.

Visiting the Meo Minority (Hmong Minority)
Ethnologists visiting Vietnam are often annoyed when they are told that they can't visit Meo villages. This can be arranged but it must be pointed out that they live in very remote mountain ranges, and horses and guides are required to get to them. Many Vietnamese ethnologists have visited them but so far as I know, no tourists. The guide at the Hoa Binh guest house knows how to get to Meo villages. If you want to go, contact Vietnam Tourism in Hanoi at least three months before your visit — you stand a chance but only a slim one I'm afraid. Don't

despair, you will probably see some of the Meo minority in the market at Hoa Binh, Son La or Dien Bien Phu. You may, if you are lucky, see White Hmong, Black Hmong, Blue Hmong and Flowered Hmong. The Hmong people are instantly recognisable by their wide silver buckled necklaces and wrist bracelets — some have coloured beads, The White Hmong have white skirts.

Continuing to Dien Bien Phu

The road from Hoa Binh to Son La gets rougher the further you go towards Son La. You will pass through rugged mountain scenery and nearer to Son La, cross the Nam Chien river. The main tourist attraction in Son La is the old prison built in 1908. Before this in the 1890s each district had a detention house called a *buon mut* (dark house) in the Thai language. This penitentiary was the site of prison riots; many escaped to Laos. The leader of the revolt, Khat (an ex-Thai corporal), was later caught and executed. Son La is also known for a big insurrection which took place five years after the riots, in which many chiefs of the Black Thai minority stormed the area and killed the French administrator, Lambat. Many beheadings took place at Son La in 1917, some were important Thai chiefs who had rebelled against French occupation.

The guest house at Son La is extremely basic and burning a mosquito coil at night is recommended.

The roughest part of the journey is from here through B Bon, Thuan Chau, Muong Ang across the N Khoa river to Muong Phan and then towards Dien Bien Phu. Dien Bien Phu is in Lai Chau province and lies between Muong Lay and Muong Te districts in the north and northwest, and Lao frontier in the south and west. Dien Bien Phu is in the Muong Thanh valley on the route through to Laos. A natural barrier, Phu Xam Xan, 1,897 metres high, blocks the valley off from Laos. The narrow valleys making up Muong Thanh are crossed by tributaries of the Ma river which runs down through Son La and Thanh Hoa. There are also tributaries of the Nam Muc and Nam Nua. Locals can boat between Dien Bien Phu and Lai Chau.

In ancient times caravans of hundreds of horses used to pass through the area on their way to Laos, Burma and China. Dien Bien Phu is a haven for ethnologists. The main minorities which are sometimes seen in the area are the Thai, Luy, Tay, Meo, Khmu, Ha Nhi, Phu La, Coong, Xingmul and Zao. Don't expect to see all of these, you will be lucky to see two or three during your short stay. Ethnologists should arrange to have three days in Dien Bien Phu.

In Dien Bien Phu you can visit the A1 mountain where there is a plan of the battle of Dien Bien Phu. Hill A1 was the most important of the five hills protecting the central part of the Dien Bien Phu stronghold. A battle was fought here from the 30th March to 4th April 1954. It was the most difficult position to take in the stronghold area.

By 9th April it still had not been completely taken and because of reinforcement by paratroopers, it was unconquered for another four days. The museum in Dien Bien Phu is dominated by a statue of Ho Chi Minh. It tells the story of the French occupation of Vietnam and the battle of Dien Bien Phu.

The battle of Dien Bien Phu

Tourists going to Dien Bien Phu should certainly know something of what the battle was all about. This simple summary of the French involvement in Vietnam will serve as a reminder.

The aggression between France and Vietnam began by the bombardment of Danang in 1858. Between the period of 1884, when the Pate Notre treaty was signed, and 1893, there had been many resistance battles against French occupation of Vietnam. The rebel king Ham Nghi had no desire to be ruled by French colonists and, assisted by Ton Thay Thuyet, set up armed resistance. He was followed by king Dong Khanh, who the French manipulated to a great degree. In 1888 the French took control of the northwest region including the upper basin of the Red River, Black River, and Ma River. Lai Chau had been taken by the French and this was followed by Son La, Hoa Binh and finally Dien Bien Phu. The minorities had fought bravely to prevent colonisation by the French. The Muong invaded Hoa Binh and the Black Thai, Son La. They were driven off to the Dien Bien Phu area where a fierce battle prevailed.

The Meo tribesmen, who were itinerant farmers on the high mountains, had joined the resistance against the French in 1864. In 1918 there was a massive Meo uprising but the French soldiers, with their superior weaponry, fought them off. Resistance to French colonial rule continued for 38 years during the late 19th Century and early 20th Century.

On September 2nd 1945 President Ho Chi Minh stated through The Declaration of Independence that Vietnam would be free. Hardly 30 days had passed before new troubles flared up in Saigon, instigated by the French and helped by the British. The trouble began to spread all over Vietnam. In December 1946 the French took Haiphong and soon after massive fighting broke out in Hanoi. A series of campaigns against the French were instigated in the 1951–52 period which liberated many areas from their control.

The guerrilla assistance in northern and southern provinces set the scene for further independence. Eight years of heavy fighting had matured the Vietnamese army, local forces had grown stronger and guerrilla activity had increased. The weaponry used had improved a great deal and the determination of the people to die for Ho Chi Minh's independence policy carried an iron conviction. Despite the increasing US aid to the French forces, the morale of the Vietnamese soldiers never faltered. During 1953 the French suffered bad defeats in

Laos and, determined that the same thing wouldn't happen in Vietnam, increased their strength by mustering up a strong 'puppet army.' American dollars flooded to their aid. The French General Navarre succeeded in many attacks: Lang Son in July 1953, Ninh Binh and Thanh Hoa provinces in October 1953. On the 20th November 1953, six hand picked battalions were parachuted into the Muong Thanh plain to occupy Dien Bien Phu. Navarre's troops were to reinforce the area and later to move towards Son La. Dien Bien Phu was thought to be an unassailable fortress. In the meantime General Giap's seasoned army were moving in on the area. Lai Chau town was liberated from the French on December 12th 1953 and, at the same time, others were encircling Dien Bien Phu. The Vietnamese realised that the French and Americans wanted the stronghold to use it as an important base for launching offensives against northern Vietnam, upper Laos and southwest china. The north Vietnamese army, by smashing the base, could prevent the war expanding. The order for the attack on Dien Bien Phu came on March 13th 1954. By now the Vietnamese forces had been strengthened by others heading out of Laos. The main resistance centres in the Dien Bien Phu area were heavily shelled, Him Lam on March 13th, Doc Lap Hill on March 14th, and Ban Keo on March 17th. This resulted in a break in the French defence line.

The next stage of the offensive included attacking the central section of the Muong Thanh plain which had been reinforced on March 14th and 16th by two battalions from Hanoi. This area was protected by five resistance areas, the strongest being A1 hill. By the 19th April it had been taken. The end was near for the French General De Casties and his remaining 10,000 troops. They were completely demoralised and on May 7th white flags appeared in the central sector. The General surrendered. It was the greatest victory ever for Giap's troops and, with the signing of the Geneva agreement on July 21st 1954, peace returned to Indochina — for a short time.

Hanoi to Haiphong

This trip is usually orgainsed by the Tourist Authority although I have heard of a few journalists who have managed to take the train. Normally tourists are not allowed to do this. The road for Haiphong leaves Hanoi over the Soaring Dragon Bridge aptly named after the name for ancient Hanoi, Thang Long. Photographs of this bridge are strictly forbidden.

Scores of new houses are being built, particularly in the area of the steam train factory. Steam trains packed solid with people, merchandise, even chickens and ducks, pass near the roadside where huge pots, agricultural produce and even large furniture is carried on bicycles.

Along the route there is an occasional turkey farm and scores of duck herders with long bamboo canes with a cloth at the end. Brick-making kilns bellow out their dark smoke, and laden buffalo carts transport bricks to the nearest rail stop at Haiduong. Brick factories have sprung up everywhere to cope with the massive demands for rebuilding programmes.

This stretch was heavily bombed during the war and thousands of new residences have been rebuilt. Many have their rebuilding dates clearly marked on the front, 1985, 1986 and 1987. The main road leading into Haiphong has many industrial complexes, cement works, engineering factories, shipyards, glassworks and lime kilns. It is fascinating to watch limestone being carried up helter skelter pathways to the tops of lime kilns where large stones are dumped into the apex of the furnace. The traffic on the Cam river is always pretty heavy.

The city of Haiphong is reached in about two hours from Hanoi (102km).

Bullock cart near Haiduong

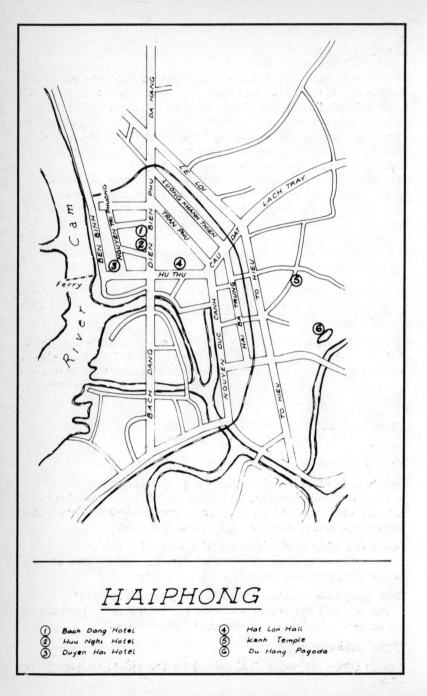

HAIPHONG

① Bach Dang Hotel
② Huu Nghi Hotel
③ Duyen Hai Hotel
④ Hat Lon Hall
⑤ Kenh Temple
⑥ Du Hang Pagoda

HAIPHONG

This is one of the biggest cities in Vietnam having over one million inhabitants. It lies in the northeast of the Bac Bo delta, on the left bank of the Cam river. It is now a commercial docking area for ships of up to 10,000 tons. The port has been massively dredged to clear it from bombs and old war mines. During French occupation the bed of the Cam river was insufficiently dredged, ships of over 5,000 tons then had to be unloaded by barges in Ha Long Bay.

Haiphong was badly damaged during the Vietnam war by bombs, shells and mines. The growth of the city's industrial quarter mushroomed after French withdrawal, which gives it a somewhat non-touristy image. There are attractive parts to the city including the main store area on Dien Bien Phu street where a very elegant theatre and rows of stalls make good subjects for the photographer. The markets thrive with activity.

Fish market   This specialises in selling unusual sea produce, such as turtles, *tu hai* fish and abalones. The best time to visit is very early morning when the stock is arriving.

Crafts   Haiphong is a good place to buy souvenirs. There are woollen and rush carpets, brass and cast-iron figures, pumice, lacquer and pearl incrustations, articles made from tortoise shells, buffalo horns, and jute tapestries. All can be bought for modest prices from the shops opposite theatre square.

Tourist Facilities — Haiphong

Hotels
There are three main tourist hotels.

Huu Nghi 55 Dien Bien Phu, Haiphong. Tel: 47206.
This has 30 rooms, 14 are air conditioned. Services include restaurant, souvenir shop and laundry. The rooms are priced from US$20/ night which is very expensive for this class of hotel.

Duyen Hai 5 Nguyen Tri Phuong, Haiphong. Tel: 47657.
It has 30 rooms all air conditioned. Services are the same as above but on Thursdays and Saturdays there is a dance.

Bach Dang Hotel 40 Dien Bien Phu, Haiphong. Tel: 47244.
This has only five rooms which are air conditioned. There are two restaurants, a bar, souvenir shop and laundry service.

Other addresses
Tourist Office Haiphong Tourism, 15 Le Dai Hanh, Haiphong. Tel: 47486.

Viet-Tiep Hospital, Duong Cat Da, Haiphong.

Foreign Trade Bank, Duong Nguyen Tri Phuong, Haiphong.

Post Office 3 Nguyen Tri Phuong, Haiphong.

Excursions

Wood carving village of Bao Ha   The art of statue carving has been well known in this village for several centuries. It was founded by Nguyen Cong Hue who lived in the late 17th and early 18th Centuries. A very famous statue carved by him is kept at the Ba Xa temple at Bao Ha. After his death his students erected a temple for him and produced a statue of Nguyen Cong Hue which was painted red.

A favourite wood used by the carvers is jackwood which is light, soft, beautiful and fragrant. The village craftsmen concentrate on carving religious statues but also produce carvings of animals such as buffalo, lion, phoenix and dragon. All the work is of an extremely high standard, only very modest prices are charged.

Hang Kenh Communal House   This is an ancient architectural work dedicated to Ngo Quyen, a national hero credited with consolidating Vietnam's independence in the 10th Century. This house is made of wood with sophisticated carvings, some of them arranged in three-tiered panels.

Boat ride   Visitors can go on the Bach Dang river where Vietnamese national heroes led the people's forces to defeat many invader armies.

Don Son   This is a seaside resort with comfortable hotels nestled amidst pine trees. There are miles of sandy beaches. This resort is normally only visited by Vietnamese tourists.

Duhang Temple   This is in Le Chan district and is dedicated to Le Chan, a talented woman general of the Trung sisters (1st Century AD). This temple is undoubtedly the most ornate in Haiphong. There are two guardians near the entry to the inner enclosure, one bad, one good. The magnificent central altar has an elaborately carved offerings table over which hangs a spiral joss-stick burner. Beyond is the baby Buddha surrounded by nine dragons. Behind are the Buddhas of the past, present and future. The stone stelae at the rear of the temple commemorate the temple keepers.

Visit to a water puppet show   I am told that these still occur around the Haiphong area but they are extremely difficult to locate (see section on Thay pagoda). Infrequent performances occur at the puppet guild Nhan Hoa (Vinh Bao district).

From Haiphong the visitor can travel on to Thai Binh or to Halong Bay.

Haiphong to Thai Binh

Very few tourists ever go to Thai Binh. If you have time the Tourist
Authority can be persuaded to take you.

The journey involves three bridge crossings, so no photographs are
allowed in these locations. The four ferry crossings slow down the
journey but they are excellent places to meet the locals. The countryside is very rich in produce, judging from the variety of vegetables
brought onto the ferries. Many women carry huge baskets of tapioca
on their heads, others have cabbages, lettuces, potatoes, parsnips and
peas.

Fishing villages

There are scores of fishing villages along this route, many have huge
aerial nets suspended from bamboo poles. Local markets display large
varieties of fish in large reed baskets. There is a rumour that Russian
oil exploration firms are moving into the area and one wonders what
this will do to the eco-systems. The piles of stone looking like
decapitated towers on the roadside are the remains of machine gun
towers used by the French.

This province is one of the richest of the North. Rice fields are
everywhere and the yields are reported to be very high.

Thai Binh Town

This was badly damaged during the war. The whole area is remarkably
flat, not a single mountain is visible. The tourist hotel is still only
partially built. Not many people stay here for the night anyway, they
normally go back to Haiphong or on to Nam Dinh. There are,
however, some interesting visits to be made in the town:

Carpet factory   This contains around 350 staff, mostly women. It was
opened in 1973 and specialises in floral wool carpets which are sold to
Eastern bloc countries and the Soviet Union. The chairwoman of the
factory will invite foreign guests to drink tea and tell them about the
factory's achievements. Its well worth going even though everything is
in three small rooms.

The museum   This depicts general history including some prehistoric
exhibits. There are exhibits dedicated to the sisters Bat Gan and Dyen
Ha who survived insurrection attempts against Chinese aggressors in
the province. The story of General Ba Vanh's struggle against the
Nguyen kings is told. He led a massive peasant rebellion in the 17th
Century.

There are distressing pictures of the famine in Thai Binh in the 1940s
and the war against the French. Paintings are exhibited which show
agricultural improvement. The photographs are of young liberation
fighters. Finally the pictures of damage inflicted to the area during the
Vietnam war are disturbing.

Visit to Dong Sam in Thai Binh Province

There are two reasons for visiting Don Sam village. The first is that it contains a temple dedicated to Tran Hung Dao, the national hero who defeated the Chinese in the 13th Century. The second is to see the master goldsmiths at work.

According to the chairman of the cooperative, Do Xuan Thu, a person cannot master the art until they have been working at it for 20 years. All his students take four or five years even to learn the rudiments. The grand master of this art is Nguyen Tung who is 88 years old.

The art was first introduced 500 years ago by Nguyen Kim Lau. Even before the end of the first Indochina war (1954) exquisitely tooled products were exported to Korea, France, China and Canada.

They specialise in gold-rimmed plates, scabbards, Buddhist figures, animals such as dragon, tiger, turtle, phoenix and bat, together with fruit clusters made of solid gold. Since 1965 bronze articles have also been manufactured.

Back to Haiphong

After the visits in Thai Binh province the same road is taken back to Haiphong. It is not a very interesting place to spend the night but it is worth seeing if there is anything on at the local theatre. They sometimes have Cheo performances.

Journey to Halong Bay

It is best to make a very early start since the scenery en route is very spectacular. To leave Haiphong travellers must take the ferry across the estuary of a branch of the Red River. This is usually crammed with cars, trucks and bicycles and in the port of Haiphong, large ships from Cuba, Sweden, Denmark and the Soviet Union are docked. No photography allowed in the port.

The ferry crosses to the area where old Chinese-style junks are moored on the opposite bank. Peasants carrying pineapples on their heads, melons, bananas, pigs in conical baskets, and quacking ducks strapped to their bicycles, scramble to be first off. From here there is another ferry crossing before you will see the idyllic panoramas at the approach to Halong Bay.

Halong Bay

According to an ancient legend, when Vietnam was attacked by foreign forces a long time ago, God sent a mother dragon and her sons to protect the Vietnamese. The dragon split many mountains of stone to impede the progress of the enemy. The big rocky island is called Ha Long (where the mother dragon landed), the smaller islands are called Bai Tu Long (sons of dragons) and another group of small islands is called Long Vi (dragon's tails).

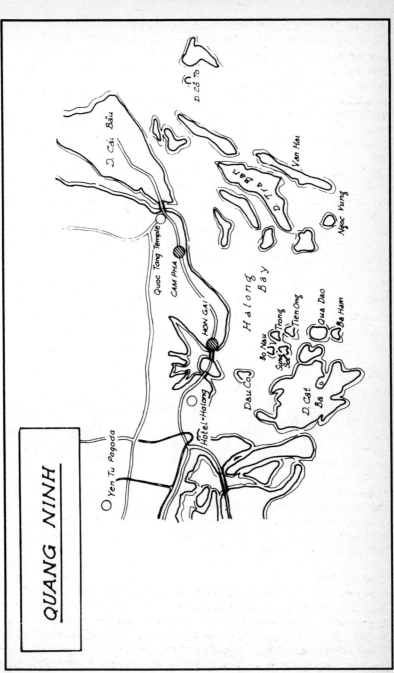

The best panoramic view of Halong Bay is obtained from the coal mining town of Hongai. Some of the islets have been described by Vietnamese poets as being like fighting cocks, men's heads, frogs, turtles and dragons.

In the early morning the brown and white sails of the fishing fleet can

A jagged karst landscape in Halong Bay.

be seen silhouetted against the karstic island chain. In its deep waters are holothurians, abalones, lobsters, cuttlefish and shrimps.

An island known as Dau-Go or Giau-Go is where wooden stakes were lit which were used to trap a Mongol fleet as they sailed down the Bach Dang river. Inside the limestone formations are natural sculptures of buffaloes, horses and elephants. Tourists can sail for 2 km through the Hang Manh tunnel and observe rocks in the shape of stupas and household jars. The souvenir shops of Hon Gai sell black coal sculptures of the area together with shells and coral.

Other visits in the vicinity of Halong Bay

Cat Ba National Park This is 60 km east of Haiphong and has just opened to tourism. It has 620 plant species including the precious tree,

Kim Giao, nearly 100 species of birds, amphibians, weasels, porcupines, wild cats, monkeys and gibbons. There are many interesting caves on the island.

Yen Tu Mountain   This is 50 km from the township. Apart from the beautiful scenery, there is a temple dedicated to King Tran Nhan Tong and the two monks Phap Loa and Huyen Quang. These were founders of a rare form of Buddhism called Truc Lam. There are a variety of minority groups in the area: Tay, Dao, Hoa and San Chi, which cannot be visited without special permission.

Dai Khi Island   Monkeys are bred here for export. Some are used in medical establishments as experimental animals for the production of a vaccine against poliomyelitis.

Tourist Facilities — Quang Ninh — Halong Bay

Hotels

All foreign visitors stay in the hotel overlooking Bai Chay beach. This is in fact a complex of three hotels, **Halong**, **Bach Long** and **Son Long**. There are 500 beds and the facilities include restaurant, laundry service, video and bar. Beer seems to be difficult to get at this hotel. You can easily buy some by walking down to the beach where there are vendors selling beer at inflated prices. It's a lovely tranquil place to stay with a magnificent view of the bay.

Hai Long — *Floating Hotel*
   This is just for Vietnamese tourists.

Other tourist facilities

Tourist Office Duong Bai Chay, Thi Xa, Quang Ninh. Tel: 08 Quang Ninh.

Hospital Duong Lan Be, Thi Xa, Hon Gai, Quang Ninh.

Post Office Duong Bai Chay.

Bank Ben Doan, Thi Xa, Hon Gai.

Cinema and Theatre Workers Culture House, Duong Ben Doan, Thi Xa, Hon Gai.
Cinema Ha Long, Thi Xa, Hon Gai.

FROM HANOI TO NINH BINH

Many tourists from Hanoi visit the Cuc Phuong forest where new recreational sites have been developed in the national park. The road to Phuly often runs alongside the Hanoi to Ho Chi Minh railway line. The long distance trains are diesel but the ones running to Ninh Bihn and Thanh Hoa are often steam.

The landscape is totally dominated by distant karst peaks in a limstone wilderness. Many are said to contain the remains of primitive man. They are honeycombed with huge underground tunnels containing fresh mineral water. Many limestone quarries and lime kilns are dotted throughout the province. Cranes load huge chunks of limestone into tall towers where they are fired to produce valuable lime dust. This is mixed with cement and sand and used by the building industry. Large shipments go to Hanoi, Hue, Danang and Ho Chi Minh.

For at least 50 km from Phuly to Ninh Binh the road is covered with piles of paddy rice. A lot of the cooperatives still thresh it by allowing vehicles to run over it again and again. Alongside fields with triangular rice stacks, duck herders move their flocks away from approaching traffic.

The massive cooperatives, some having 400 family members, cultivate huge rice fields on a contract system. They produce a certain amount of rice for the cooperative which is government sold and the proceeds go towards upkeep of the cooperative, and for wages. Any amount of rice produced above the fixed quota is sold by the peasants. This form of land reform has encouraged intensive farming techniques using artificial fertilisers and has increased the yield per hectare immensely.

There is a huge limestone quarry on the side of the road just before Ninh Binh.

Hoa Lu — the ancient capital of Vietnam

For travellers to Ninh Binh in Ha Nam Ninh province, the highlight of the visit will be a visit to Hoa Lu, the ancient capital of Vietnam from 968 to 1010. Two important temples can be visited in the area: the temple of King Dinh Tien Hoan (968–980), and the temple of King Le Hoan (980–1009).

Some History

The original Hoa Lu Citadel was built in a narrow karstic valley which was easy to defend. According to ancient scripts, it was guarded by tigers and panthers. The original structure was built of precious woods, *trai*, *nghien*, *cochi*, *lat hoa*, and *kim giao* which grew on the Ma Yen or Nui Yen Ngua mountains.

In his younger days King Dinh Tien Hoang was called Dinh Bo Linh. He lived in the valley with his uncle Dinh Thuc Du. At an early age the elders of the village recognised that he was destined to become a great leader. Later during his military life he had many victories against his greatest enemies the Ngo family, Phong and Kieu Cong Han.

The Temple of King Dinh Tien Hoang

The temple which is managed by Mr Duong Van Bai was built in the 11th Century. It is entered via an outer triumphant arch, Nghi Mon

Ngoai, and then an inner triumphant gate, Nghi Mon Noi. When it was originally built, it faced towards the north. In 1696 it was rebuilt and now faces east.

In the centre of the courtyard in front of the main building is the Dragon Bed, once an area for sacrifices. During festivals such as the festival of the reed flags (see *Festivals in the North*), food, gifts and cakes are put onto the slab. Either side of the temple are mythical animals with the head of a lion and the body of a dog.

Inside the Temple   The central altar is for the worship of King Dinh Tien Hoang. The large old Vietnamese characters read 'From this day on we have our independence'. The flamingoes standing on the backs of tortoises are considered to be the symbols of saints and the tortoises the symbol of long life. The writing on the pillars in ancient Vietnamese translates as 'Dai Co Viet', the name Dinh Bo Linh gave to Vietnam. On the other pillar is written 'Hoa Lu is prosperous as the capital of ancient Vietnam'.

The statues in the back room   The central figure covered in dust is the King Dinh Bo Linh. His three sons are also represented. The left statue (i.e. right facing) is Dinh Quoc Lien, his eldest son. He held the second highest position to his father in the Hoa Lu Court. On the other side of the King are the statues of Dinh Hang Lang and Dinh Toan.

Dinh Hang Lang in the first months of 978, had been proclaimed heir apparent. Lien, who was not about to let his inheritance be stolen, had early in 979 sent an assassin to kill Dinh Hang Lang. Near the end of that year an official named Do Tich assassinated the King and his eldest son. It is reported that when caught he was beheaded and his flesh fed to the people. Dinh's third son then became King Dinh Toan when he was only six years old. He, sadly, had a short rule, only four months, then General Le Hoan was crowned king by the Hoa Lu Court.

The Le Hoan Temple
This is a miniature of the Dinh Hoang temple. Inside the altar arrangement is similar. In the back room are statues of the General King Le Hoan with the mother Queen Duong Van Nga on his left (right facing). On the right side (left facing) are the King's sons Le Long Dinh, who died at the age of 24, and Le Long Viet his elder brother.

The Pagoda in the Mountains
This is an unusual three tier pagoda rebuilt by two monks, Chi Kien and Chi The. It can be reached by road or by boat. By boat it is quite a long trip, around three hours, along meandering narrow channels through rice green fields surrounded by peculiar shaped karst peaks. The boats transport the visitor under three caverns where huge

stalactites hang from the roof. From the docking point it is about a one and a half kilometre walk to the temple.

The Ninh Binh Area
The countryside is totally idyllic, huge limestone promontories stretch as far as the horizon. In the early morning limestone carts hauled by buffalo transport their cargoes to lime kilns. As the evening falls oil lamps burn in the shop windows and the town is filled with the glow from the windows and the town is filled with the glow from the lime kilns.

Tourist Facilities — Ha Nam Ninh Province

Hotels
In Ninh Binh: Hoa Lu, Huyen Hoa Lu, Ha Nam Ninh, Thi Xa, Ninh Binh. Tel: 39 Hoa Lu.

This is a very small hotel with 34 beds. It is being rebuilt in parts. The restaurant serves excellent food but foreigners are usually put in a different room from their driver and interpreter. The laundry service is efficient but the charge is usually in dollars (very expensive). The staff are tremendously friendly. The rooms tend to have a lot of insects in them and at night you can be kept awake by the sound of wood-boring beatles. Despite its bad points, it's one of my favourite hotels in the northern provinces.

In Nam Dinh: Vi Hoang Hotel, 115 Nguyen Du, Thi Xa, Nam Dinh. Tel: 290.

This has 39 rooms, only two are air-conditioned with attached bathroom. The services include three restaurants, video and laundry.

Other addresses in Nam Dinh
Tourist Office 115 Nguyen Du, Thi Xa, Nam Dinh. Tel: 439.

Post Office Duong Ha Huy Tap, Thi Xa, Nam Dinh. Tel: 332 or 232.

Bank Duong Tran Hung Dao, Thi Xa, Nam Dinh. Tel: 438

Hospital Benh Vien 1, Duong Tran Quoc Toan, Thi Xa, Nam Dinh. Tel: 223.

Bookshop Duong Hoang Van Thu, Thi Xa, Nam Dinh. Tel: 516.

Theatre Rap Binh Minh, Duong Tran Hung Dao, Nam Dinh. Tel: 788.

Points of interest around Nam Dinh
Textile mill Special permission from the authorities in Hanoi is required to visit this.

Museum of the province Not of much interest to western visitors.

Thien Truong Temple (My Loc district) This is a very run down dilapidated place. It is dedicated to the 14 kings of the Tran Dynasty (13th–14th Century). It commemorates their victories against the Mongols in the 13th Century. During the 13th and 14th Century this place was considered to be the second imperial capital (after Thang Long).

Pho Minh Pagoda The pagoda was built in 1262 and the tower in 1308. It is dedicated to the King Tran Nhan Tong who, having transferred the crown to his son Tran Anh Tong, came to live in this pagoda.

He, together with two Buddhist monks Phap Loa and Huyen Quang, founded the Truc Lam branch of Buddhism. When Tran Nhan Tong died, he was cremated and the ash was made into 21 small balls, seven of which were stored on top of the tower in the grounds of the pagoda.

Travelling through Thanh Hoa Province

Between Ninh Binh and Thanh Hoa is a good place to see steam trains. The railway line which runs very close to the road in places, was built mostly during the 1936–1941 period although it was started around 1901. During the wars against the French and Americans it was badly damaged. The bridges on this stretch were all destroyed.

This journey passes over the famous Ham Rong bridge which spans the Song Ma river. During the Vietnamese war this was the most heavily defended area in North Vietnam. For three years from 1965 it was pounded by over 100 air attacks and finally destroyed by "smart" bombs in 1972. During the 2nd Century the province was the home of the famous female general Trieu Thi Trinh, who fought against the Chinese. It was also the military headquarters of the King Le Loi and the talented strategist Nguyen Trai during the struggle against the Ming in the 15th Century. The province is now famous for its sugar-cane plantations and duck farms.

TRAVELLING THROUGH NGHE TINH PROVINCE

On entering this province, travelling down highway Number One from Thanh Hoa, a distinct difference is noticed from the terrain of the upper delta. The coastal plains of the province stretch from the southern lands below the Chu river to the Transversal or Ngang Pass through the Hoanh Son mountains. The area of land, which extends from the 20th to the 18th parallel, starts 400 km south of Hanoi.

More and more tourists are now making the journey overland. After crossing the border from Thanh Hoa province they head for the town of Quynh Luu along highway Number One which runs very close to the railway. It is not uncommon to see steam trains in the Hoang Mai region, just after crossing the border. Sadly, the train between Ho Chi Minh and Hanoi is now diesel. Quynh Luu is on the southern side of the Tinh Gia chain of hills where two rice crops a year are harvested in the lower regions and sweet potatoes and groundnuts flourish higher up. The state has poured what little money is spare into improving mechanisation. A new tractor station has been built, roads have improved and agricultural devlopment has increased.

Off limits Further over towards the northwest in the Phu Quy area of Nghia Dan is rich basaltic soil where plantations of rubber, coffee and oranges flourish. This area and the road from Dien Chau to Ky Son (Muong Xen) are currently off limits to western tourists. The authorities say the roads are very bad in places and there is no suitable accommodation!

Travelling down the plain of Quynh Luu and Dien Chau the Truong Son range of mountains can be seen on the Laos border. On a clear day the peak Pu Hoat is visible. This range extends the whole length of the province from north of the Ca river to the Mu Gia pass. Tourists travelling this route in the summer months will experience the warm winds which blow inwards from Laos. Over the centuries this area of Nghia Tinh has silted up but at one time it was joined by the Hoang Mai channel to Thanh Hoa bay. Archaeolgocial evidence has indicated that Dien Chau was once a lagoon; polished stone age tools found in the area have indicated a 'lake culture'. Translated from the Vietnamese, Dien Chau means 'land of underground water', and the whole area is criss-crossed by many underground streams. Since the building of the Vach Bac hydraulic system, completed in December 1976, the Dien Chau and Yen Thanh districts have been well drained and are now suitable for growing rice, maize, and even tea and pineapples.

The Nghi Loc region lying on the central plains had been subjected to very bad silting. The sand from the coast has moved in and now extends from Nghi Loc through Nghi Xuan and even to the Cua Lo hills. The small hamlet of Cua Lo, which very few westerners visit, is a fishing area. Nuoc Mam (fish sauce) is produced here in small quantities. Towards the northwest of Nghi Loc are the Hong Linh mountains, the home of minority people who have deforested the area by their slash and burn techniques. Towards the Laos border thick forests still flourish but it is feared that the Meo, Muong and Thai minorities in the area will eventually deforest that region too. Special government-run logging camps are responsible for reafforestation management. The timber, *mun* (ebony), *lim* (ironweed) sen and *tau* is only sparingly logged. Two new trees are planted to replace each one taken. I have heard that these forests contain leopards, tigers, elephants, deer, gibbons, and flying squirrels.

Vinh Area

The railway extending north to Hanoi was rebuilt by 1963 having been badly damaged by French aircraft before 1954. Highway Number One, which is now in good repair, was virtually destroyed during this period. Vinh, the capital of the province, was just a heap of rubble in 1954. During the period 1954–1964 big improvements occurred despite progress being slowed down by inadequate supplies of building materials, cement and bricks being available. Vinh was hit again on 5th August 1964 this time by US bombers. New buildings, schools, the electric power station and railway station were razed. Vinh really suffered during the war because it is an important strategic base for entering the south and extending into Laos along highways 7 and 8. During the 1965–1972 period it was again razed to the ground.

At Vinh, the Lam river — a branch of the Ca river — is often dangerously full because of the tributaries, the Ngan Sau, Ngan Pho, Gianh and Hieu, pouring into it. The worst time to travel in the area is September to November. It was badly hit by flooding in 1978 just after the rebuilding programme had boosted the number of industrial enterprises, handicraft industries and expanded cooperatives. Much of the cooperatives' land was covered in deep mud.

Tourist spots in Vinh

You only need one day to see Vinh. It is not one of my favourite places in Vietnam. The climate in the area is somewhat oppressive — it always seems to be raining. Visits can be arranged to:

Cho Vinh, The central market.   This is a large aircraft hangar-like building in the centre of the capital. There's not much there, certainly no tourist crafts, but the hardened travelller and photographer will find it interesting. At the back of the main building is an area for selling vegetables and sea foods — the people here are tremendously friendly and you will get some good photos.

The beach   Western visitors won't think much of the beach but it is well worth going to at about 5.30 to 6 am just before the sun comes up. Tourists staying at the Hotel Cua Lo, 20 km from Vinh town, can walk onto the beach which is just across the road. In early February I have seen the area covered for about 5 km with fishermen pulling in their nets. The nets are set very early in the morning by hardy peasants in conical boats; by sunrise they are ready to draw them in. The nets glisten with long silver eel-like fish. This makes a marvellous spectacle for photographers, especially if there is a good sunrise.

The theatre   This is well worth going to. It's over the road from the Chuyen Gia Giao Te hotel. There are often acrobatic performances and traditional theatre. **Warning:** Once the show has started you can't

get out. Metal gates are locked at the entrance (a considerable fire
hazard) to prevent gate-crashers. You will find it very amusing to see
the audience and their reaction to westerners especially if you intend
taking photographs during the performance! The Theatre (workers
cultural house), Nha Van Hoa Lao Dong, is in Duong Minh Khai. Tel:
2377.

Ho Chi Minh's native residence   He was born west of Vinh on 19th
May 1890 in the village of Chua. From six years old he lived in Sen, the
native village of his father. Life in the area has always been notoriously
hard. The people raise silkworms, weave silk fabrics, make cooking
pots. Many go far into the mountains to gather wood to make
charcoal. The two houses in Sen and Chua villages have become an
historical site, many Vietnamese visit them but very few westerners.
Outside the residence where he was born a sign in Vietnamese states
that bicycles and inflammables are not allowed in the grounds and that
visitors should keep off the flower beds. The thatch-roofed house
nestles in the centre of Kim Lien commune. His mother, Hoang Thi
Loan, brought him into the world on a bamboo bed given to her by her
father on her marriage. The boy was called Nguyen Sinh Cung (it was
later that he was known as Ho Chi Minh). When he was six he moved
to the village of Sen to a house which had been presented to his father
by the local people after he had received the degree of Pho Bang
(Doctor of Literature) at Hue. His mother died in 1901 when he was
only 11 years old. His father, Nguyen Sinh Sac, encouraged his
education and it wasn't long before Cung decided to devote his life to
the cause of national liberation. He returned to Hue and studied at
Dong Ba Franco primary school and later at Quoc Hoc National High
School. He left Hue in 1910 under a new name, Nguyen Tat Thanh,
and travelled the world to discover a way of liberating his nation.

Visitors to Ho Chi Minh's native residence will see his writing desk,
books, wooden trunk and kitchen cupboard where he kept his toys.
The wooden and bamboo house where the President grew up was
dismantled when his father moved to Hue in 1905. In 1955 the house
was rebuilt by the local population as an exact replica.

Although he returned to Vietnam in 1941, Ho Chi Minh didn't
return to his childhood village until 15th June 1957 and again on 9th
December 1961.

The visitor will see that there have been big improvements to the
Nam Lien commune which is now part of a cooperative. The people of
Sen have even built a museum displaying photographs of his illustrious
life.

It is well worth requesting to see a school in Vinh. The tourist
authority encourages this since many new ones have been built since
the end of the war.

Tourist Facilities — Vinh
Hotels
The best is undoubtedly the **Chuyen Gia Giao Te**, Thanh Ho, Vinh. Tel: 4175.

It is a very large hotel mostly used for Vietnamese people and Eastern Bloc visitors. It has 180 beds in 90 rooms, 25 rooms have air-conditioning (fans and wall mounted units). Services include a restaurant which serves excellent Vietnamese food, laundry, video and table tennis. Tourists are advised to pay their laundry bills in dong — although the staff may insist on dollars!

Hotel Cua Lo — A beach 20 km from Vinh. Tel: Cua Lo 13.

This is practically always deserted. Half of the rooms are air-conditioned. There are 48 available but every time I have been there I have been the only guest. The restaurant is massive especially when you, your driver and interpreter are the only people using it. The staff are very kind but the food is rather basic. They have a laundry service but hardly anyone stays there long enough to pick it up.

Other addresses
Tourist Office — Duong Quang Trung, Thanh Pho, Vinh. Tel: 4692.

Post Office — Duong Minh Khai, Thanh Pho, Vinh.

Bank — near Cho Vinh — but phone first to see if it is open! Tel: 4797–4547. (You will have no chance of changing travellers cheques in Vinh, even American Express. Low denomination dollars cash is required — don't forget your declaration form.)

Hospital — Vietnam Balan Hospital, Thanh Pho, Vinh. Tel: 4128.

Bookshop — Duong Quang Trung, Thanh Pho, Vinh. Tel: 4561.

Cinema — RAP 12/9, Duong Quang Trung, Thanh Pho, Vinh. Tel: 4984. Who knows, they may have an American film with Vietnamese subtitles or a Russian film with Vietnamese subtitles.

Vinh to the Ngang Pass
Leaving Vinh by Highway Number One built through the Ngan Sau valley, the road runs parallel with the railway for only a short distance. This valley runs in a north-south direction forming a corridor stretching through to Binh Tri Thien province. The soil is very poor around the narrow plain of Can Loc where winds blowing in from the sea bring sand which often forms high banks near the roadside. The plain of Kyanh is reached via Thach Ha, Hatinh, and Cam Xuyen. The road crosses the river Lac Giang and heads between the hills of Cua Nhung and Cua Khau. Only wild grass known as *rhodomyrty* will grow here. Towards the Ngang Pass sand banks glisten a vivid yellow in the fading sunlight. The Hoanh Son range soon comes into sight. This natural

barrier which shields Binh Tri Thien province from the northern winds
once constituted the southern border of ancient Vietnam which it
separated from the kingdom of Champa. Later it constituted the
division point between the Trinh lords in the north and the Nguyen in
the south.

A brief history of Nghe Tinh Province

Archaeological evidence has shown that a bronze age culture existed
here. During the period of the Hung kings 4,000 years ago, it was
inhabited by tribes of Van Lang. Mai Thuc Loan is well remembered
in the province for ousting the Chinese in 772. From the 10th Century
onwards Nghe Tinh constituted the southernmost part of the country
bordering Champa. The Mongols invaded the area in 1285 and in 1426
it was an important base for Le Loi and Nguyen Trai's march on Dong
Quan (now Hanoi). Between 1627–1672 it became a battlefield for the
rival Trinh lords from the north and the Nguyen family from the south.
During the 18th Century it formed an important strategic base for
Nguyen Hue, the leader of the Tay Son revolt. The whole country rose
up against the French invasion during which Le Ninh from Nghe Tinh
province is remembered for his courage. A violent liberation struggle
raged against the French culminating in the 1930 peasant revolts.
During the 1946–1954 anti-French resistant period the French were
defeated on the Lo river. 1952 marked the period of severe French
aggression in the province — they bombed Highway Number One and
destroyed many dams and sluices. The 'scorched earth' policy saw
Vinh burnt to the ground by its own inhabitants rather that let the
French capture it.

The province then went through a period of peaceful reconstruction
from 1954–1964, but the period 1964–1968 saw the aero-naval war in
full swing. Vinh was attacked by US planes on 5th August 1964. From
the 7th February 1965 the bombing of the north moved further south
and, in May, Nghe Tinh became a prime target. A second period of
intense bombing followed between April 1972 and January 1973.

Old woman, Nghe Tinh Province (note black enamelled teeth).

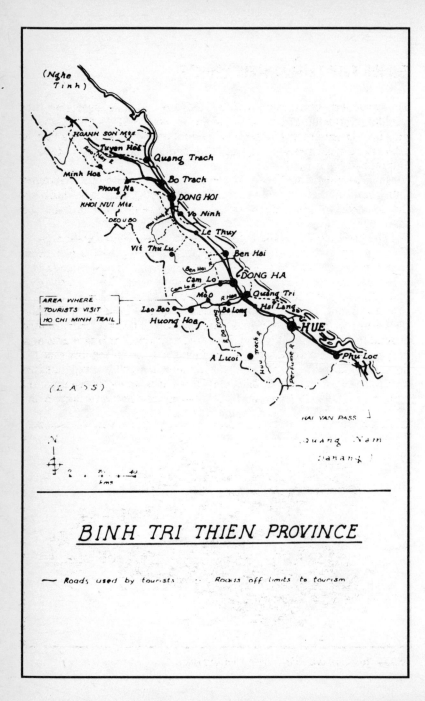

BINH TRI THIEN PROVINCE

—— Roads used by tourists   ·· Roads off limits to tourism

BINH TRI THIEN PROVINCE

The traveller enters the province just after passing over the 18th parallel region and heads for the town of Quang Trach. From here to the Hai Van mountains in the 16th parallel region is about 300km. The province is a narrow strip of land bounded on one side by mountains and on the other by the sea.

Many problems are faced by the agricultural community. Around Dong Hoi, sand blows into the rice fields from the huge sand dunes on the roadside, despite the Tamarish pines planted to hold back the sand.

The heavy rainfall in the region is highest on the mountains west of Thua Thien where there is often heavy flooding. Marine erosion sometimes occurs when sea water renders the rice fields useless. This was very marked during the Vietnam War when bombs destroyed many of the dykes in the Dong Hoi and Le Thuy areas.

Many bomb craters are being filled in but people are still being blown up by bombs dropped during the war. This is a bad problem around the 17th parallel bridge. The area near the Ben Hai river is now very productive despite the serious damage. It is remarkable that the area near Gio Linh is now used for growing pineapples, areca nuts, tea and bananas. There are still remains of old tanks, a bombed-out church at Quang Tri and many shell casings to remind visitors of the war.

A T54 Russian tank, a left-over from the war.

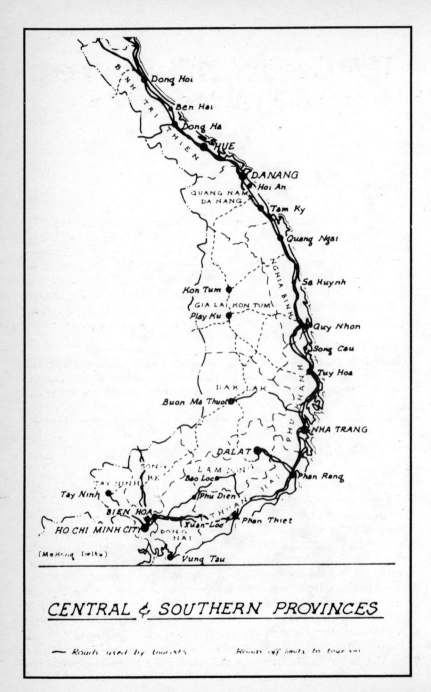

CENTRAL & SOUTHERN PROVINCES

— Roads used by tourists   Roads off limits to tourists

The Central and Southern Provinces

HUE

One of the highlights of any tour of Vietnam is a visit to Hue. This ancient capital of the Nguyen dynasty was given as a wedding present by the King of Champa to a Vietnamese princess. Lying on National Highway Number One, it is a city of pagodas, temples and royal tombs of seven of the 13 Nguyen Kings. Six hundred years ago, its foundations were built on the Perfume River at the place known as Thuan Hoa. In 1802 when the Nguyen royal dynasty was founded, it was ruled by the Emperor Gia Long and became the capital of Vietnam.

When to visit

Hue suffers more than its fair share of bad weather. In May, June and July the southern monsoons bring rain which gets very heavy in August, September and October. The wet weather often continues right through to the end of the year. Don't forget your umbrella when you go to Hue. Even at the best period, end of February to mid March, it does rain fairly often. Photographers should be warned to bring fast film as the sky is cloudy more often than not.

History

The city was invaded by the French in 1833 who ousted the young Emperor Ham Nghi from the Imperial City in 1885.

During the French rule, a quick succession of Kings replaced each other in Hue. Dong Khanh, who followed Ham Nghi, was soon replaced by Thanh Thai. His son Duy Tan, who became King when he was only eight years old reigned for a mere eight years until 1916. During this period the anti-French demonstrations brought considerable unrest, and there was little improvement during Khai Dinh's short reign from 1916–1925. The workers' strikes during 1930–1935 brought more problems for the French. Worse was to follow and in 1945, after overthrowing the French regime in Indo-China, the Japanese took control of Hue. On the 24th August 1945 the last of the Nguyen kings, Bao Dai, abdicated in the Imperial City. This was the end of the old Hue.

The relatively peaceful period from 1954, when Hue had become part of South Vietnam, ended with the anti-Buddhist propaganda sparking Buddhist demonstrations. Visitors to the Thien Mu Pagoda in Hue can see the car which took Quang Duc, a senior monk, to Ho Chi Minh City (then called Saigon) where he set fire to himself on 11th June 1963. This was a final expression of dissent against the Diem regime. Other Buddhist protest suicides followed in Hue: Thanh Quang at the Dieude Temple and others at the Tu Dam pagoda and throughout the country. The period 31st January 1968 to the end of February is well remembered; the Imperial City suffered very substantial damage during the Tet Offensive. It has never been repaired although with the help of UNESCO some restoration is now in progress.

Many tourists going to Vietnam expect to see an Imperial City at Hue, which is equal in splendour to the one at Beijing, China. I'm afraid they will be disappointed because a lot of it no longer exists. Perhaps the reason for this should be explained. On the 31st January 1968 on the great flag-tower which dominated the setting, flapped a yellow-starred flag. To the embarrassment of President Johnson and General Westmoreland this was to stand for another four weeks. During the period of 'rebel' occupation, US marines, South Korean mercenaries, and Thieu's troops had hurled everything they had many times at the Imperial City. It was even bombarded by the Seventh Gun Fleet and subjected to attacks with napalm, phosphorous bombs and toxic gases. The loss of countless invaluable historical monuments and lives was heavily questioned by the world's press at the time. One would think from this description that there would be nothing left — fortunately this is certainly not true.

The Imperial City

The city (Dai Noi) is composed of the Royal Citadel, Hoang Thanh, and the forbidden purple city, Tu Cam Thanh, behind the Thai Hoa palace. At the entrance to the Imperial City is Cua Ngo Mon, the Royal gate. This main gateway (1 on plan) was constructed in 1834 during the fourteenth year of Emperor Ming Manh. It was later damaged and repaired during the fifth year of Khai Dinh's reign in 1921. The gate is topped with belvederes and a pavilion called the Ngu Phung (The Five Phoenix building). The middle section of its roof is now covered with yellow tiles and flanking roofs with green tiles. With special permission it is possible to climb the stairs to this site from where the emperor presided over formal ceremonies. This is one of the best places for photographs of the Thai Hoa Palace.

The whole citadel is surrounded by the Kinh Thanh, the citadel walls. It was during the reign of Emperor Gia Long that the citadel walls, moat, canals and towers were built in 1805. The citadel was built on the site of eight villages. Originally built out of earth in 1818–1819,

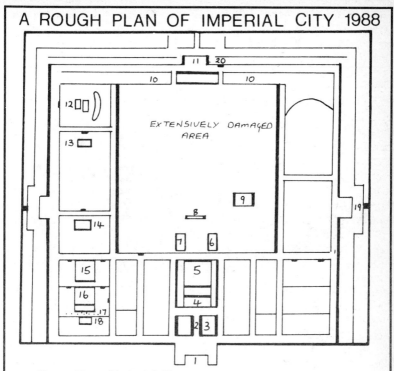

A ROUGH PLAN OF IMPERIAL CITY 1988

Key to Plan of Imperial City
 1. Ngo Mon — noontime gate
 2. Cau Trung Dao
 3. Ho Thai Dich
 4. Dai Trieu Nghi — great rites courtyard
 5. Dien Thai Hoa — throne room
 6. Huu Vu — right mandarin palace
 7. Ta Vu — left mandarin palace
 8. Bullet poxed wall of Dien Can Chanh
 9. Imperial library remains
10. Pond with water ghost shrine
11. Am Bac Dau
12. Grandmother's palace
13. King's mother's palace
14. Dien Phung temple
15. Hung Mieu temple
16. Mieu temple
17. Cuu Dinh
18. Hien Lam Cac
19. East gate
20. North gate — Hoa Binh

they were later covered with a layer of bricks two metres thick. Ten fortified gates were constructed on the four sides — some of these are in a very bad state of repair. According to ancient Chinese custom, the front of the citadel was built facing south. It is believed that between 50,000 and 80,000 men worked on the walls.

Ky Dai — The King's Knight Tower — is situated at the south wall

The main entrance gate to the Imperial City at Hue.

of the citadel. It was built under the orders of Gia Long in 1809. Originally, it was used as an observation tower by military mandarins to guard the land and sea access to the city. The tourist may be lucky enough to see the Vietnamese flag on top of the 37 m tower. It was damaged rather badly by the typhoon of 1904 but completely rebuilt by 1949. The King's Knight Tower can be seen through the archways of the Noontime Gate (Ngo Mon).

The Golden Water Bridge (2 on plan). Passing from the Noontime Gate towards the Thai Hoa Palace. The tourist will cross this bridge which is surrounded by small ponds which in turn are surrounded by frangipani blossoms. The King alone was allowed to cross this bridge.

Dai Trieu Nghi — the Great Rites Courtyard — (4 on plan). This was where the dignitaries came and paid homage to the Monarch during ceremonies. Two griffins, their canopies pocked with bullet holes, stand in solemn watch. The nine stone stelae in the courtyard divide it according to the nine mandarinate grades.

Dien Thai Hoa — The Thai Hoa Palace or Palace of Supreme Peace (5 on plan). This is where the Emperor received homage from his ministers, mandarins and military officers. The palace was built in 1805 and during the reign of Emperor Gia Long a golden throne was placed on a dais in the main hall. Only princes were allowed directly into the Throne Room. This building is completely undamaged. The ceilings and beams in the palace are lavishly decorated with red lacquer and gold inlays. The palace has been renovated by Ming Manh in 1834 and Khai Dinh in 1924.

Visitors can walk around the Thai Hoa Palace and enter the **Purple Forbidden City (Tu Cain Thanh)**. This was reserved just for the Royal Family and was protected by a wall one metre thick. Today it is largely destroyed. The palaces were damaged in 1947 and 1968. From the back of the Thai Hoa Palace the ruins of the Dien Can Chanh (8), the Heaven's Laws Palace, can be observed. This is where the King would receive his mandarins and do his daily work. The walls of the ruins which remain are bullet pocked and through an archway one can observe a large expanse of waste ground, once the site of the royal private apartments. The region was completely off limits to all aliens. The Mandarin Palaces (7) and (6) are being restored by UNESCO. Continuing through the waste ground, the remains of the Reading Book Palace (9) can be seen on the right. The visitor can walk through to the extreme northern end and turn left (10) where there is a pond. The northern gate and outer wall of the Imperial City can be seen in the distance.

Continuing left the tourist comes to the **Truong Sanh Palace** — the Grandmother's Palace (12). This lies at the northwest corner of the outer wall of the Forbidden Purple City. It was built during the reign of the Emperor Minh Mang and is now composed of three buildings together with damaged galleries. The roofs are damaged and covered by tin sheeting (1988). A few families now live in the grounds of this Palace.

Dien Tho Palace (Everlasting Longevity Palace). This Palace was built by the Emperor Gia Long in 1804. It was the residence of the Emperor's mother with facilities for privacy, some workshops, and even a room for pubic entertaining.

Passing through various gates, the visitor notices the Dien Phung Temple and Hung Mieu Temple but these are rather drab looking. The Generations Temple is worth going inside.

Generations Temple — Mieu Temple (16). This is a well preserved, very long building which houses the shrines of seven Nguyen Emperors. It wasn't until 1959 when the stelae of the three revolutionary Emperors Ham Nghi, Thanh Thai and Duy Tan were added. Some of the personal belongings are kept in the area behind the ornate altars.

Cuu Dinh (nine dynastic urns). Tourists will certainly agree that these are one of the most impressive sights in the Imperial City. The Hien Lam Cac, in front of which they stand, is undamaged. The urns were cast between 1835 and 1837 during Ming Mang's reign. They weigh between 1,900 and 2,000 kg. On the urns are figures of the sun, moon, clouds, landscapes, mountains and rivers. The largest central urn which has the most ornate scenes is dedicated to the founder of the dynasty — the Emperor Gia Long.

The Dynastic urns in front of the Hien Lam Cac.

Pagodas and tombs at Hue

Seven tombs and six pagodas may be visited by tourists in Hue: see map.

The tomb of Minh Mang

I would rate this as the most interesting of all the Imperial Tombs at Hue. It can be reached by hiring a small boat from any of the local boat people opposite the Perfume River Hotel. They will ask around 4,000 dong but with negotiation it can be brought down to 2,000. Hire a boat with a motor because a hand-rowed one will take absolutely ages to get to the tomb which is about 8 km away. An alternative but more expensive method is to use the tourist boat at the Perfume River Hotel. Most tourists on a package tour will automatically be given this facility. A car trip to the Minh Mang complex is also easy to arrange. The car takes the visitor to Ban Viet village in the Huong Tho district of Hue. From here, it is necessary to cross the river to the tomb complex. The usual charge is about 500 dong per person but I have heard that some rich looking tourists have been charged around 5,000 dong for two people. Always take an umbrella with you — it rains a lot

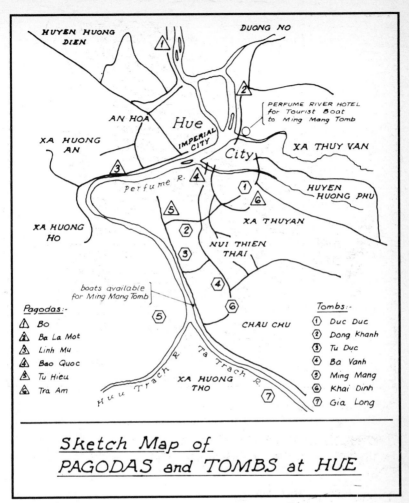

Sketch Map of
PAGODAS and TOMBS at HUE

Pagodas:-
⚠ Bo
⚠ Ba La Mot
⚠ Linh Mu
⚠ Bao Quoc
⚠ Tu Hieu
⚠ Tra Am

Tombs:-
① Duc Duc
② Dong Khanh
③ Tu Duc
④ Ba Vanh
⑤ Ming Mang
⑥ Khai Dinh
⑦ Gia Long

in Hue. It is only a short walk from where the boat docks to the Minh Mang complex.

History   During 20 years of his reign, King Minh Mang (the second king of the Nguyen dynasty), the fourth son of King Gia Long, was much respected by the local people. He encouraged advancements in agricultural techniques, built the Imperial City and reformed customs and traditions. Vietnam under Minh Mang's reign experienced much prosperity. His mausoleum was begun in 1840, one year before his death, and was finally finished by his successor King Thieu Tri in 1843.

Visitors will agree that the setting chosen for the tomb at the junction of the Ta Trach and Huu Trach tributaries of the Perfume River

PLAN OF MINH MANG TOMB HUE

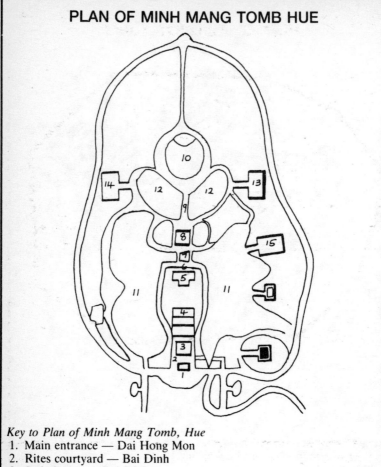

Key to Plan of Minh Mang Tomb, Hue
1. Main entrance — Dai Hong Mon
2. Rites courtyard — Bai Dinh
3. Stele house — Bai Dinh
4. Hien Duc gate
5. Dien Sung An
6. Hoang Trach Mon
7. Trung Dao bridge
8. Minh Lau temple
9. Bridge of brightness and uprightness — Cau Thong Minh Chinh Truc
10. The catacomb — Buu Thanh
11. Ho Trung Minh
12. Ho Tan Nguyet
13. Ta Tung Phong
14. Huu Tung Phong
15. Linh Phuong Cac

PLAN OF TU DUC'S TOMB

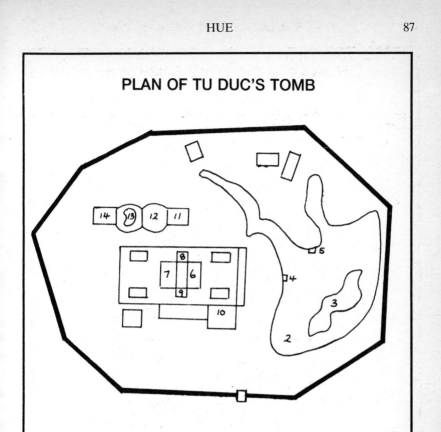

Key to Plan of Tu Duc Tomb — Hue
1. Main entrance — Cua Vu Khiem
2. Luu Khiem lake
3. Small islet — Tinh Khiem
4. Du Khiem pavilion
5. Xung Khiem pavilion
6. Hoa Khiem temple
7. Luong Khiem temple
8. Minh Khiem Duong — the theatre
9. On Khiem Duong — King's garment store
10. Chi Khiem Duong — the memorial house dedicated to concubines
11. San Chau
12. Nha Bia
13. Ho Tieu Khiem
14. Mo Vua

is just perfect. The constructions inside the complex are symmetrically set up with a distinct west-east axis (Truc Than Dao). Tourists have often commented how impressed they are with the majesty of the place, the magnificent stone carvings, and the tasteful architecture. The weatherworn parts of the complex are being restored thanks to government sponsorship. The guide will tell you that the constructions scattered in the compound symbolise the planets revolving around the earth. The place certainly has a certain charm and serenity, and undoubtedly the best time to visit is mid March when the lotus bloom in the Trung Minh and Tan Nguyet lakes. I am told that many courting couples visit the complex at that time; it certainly is a romantic place.

The tomb of Tu Duc
Getting there   This tomb is seven kilometres south west of Hue (see map). It can be easily reached by bicycle from Hue. It must be noted that it is quite difficult to hire a bicycle in Hue. The authorities don't like westerners travelling unaccompanied out of the city. Ask the receptionists at the Perfume River Hotel for advice, or better still, ask to hire their bicycles. Anyone arriving on a package tour will be provided with interpreter services and a driver. The road to the tomb passes through pine forests and a lush, hilly area to the complex which consists of 50 small constructions.

The complex took three years to build (1864–1867); over 3,000 masonry workers were involved. Some of Doan Trung's soldiers also helped and during the construction they mounted a revolt which is known as 'the uprising of the lime pestles'. Historians say that Tu Duc was a very knowledgeable and talented king but incapable of ruling the country. The complex was used as a secluded precinct during his life. In the two pavilions on the side of the lake he spent his leisure time fishing, writing poems and just contemplating the beauty of nature. The whole area was a miniature Royal Palace equipped with every facility for the king and his attendants. His grave, Buu Thanh, is now covered by a thick pine forest and on the banks of the lake are the tombs of the Queen Le Thien Anh and another simple tomb of King Kien Phu (the king's adopted son).

When the sun is shining, this poetic setting, and the decorative motifs, makes this architectural masterpiece highly rewarding.

The tomb of Khai Dinh
This can easily be reached by bicycle from Hue (see map). This king was in power for nine years (1916–1925) when Vietnam was under control of French colonists. The mausoleum took 11 years to build. Visitors to the mausoleum will be amazed how the complex resembles a European castle. It is an architectural marvel but is very blackened although it was only finished in 1931. It is not a tranquil place: the giant dragons along the staircase make it look rather sinister. The tourist will

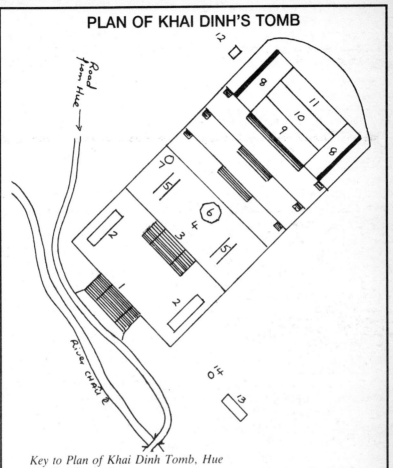

PLAN OF KHAI DINH'S TOMB

Key to Plan of Khai Dinh Tomb, Hue

1. Cua Sat — Iron gate
2. Hai Nha Ta Huu — antichambers
3. Cua Tam Quan — gate
4. San Chau — Rites courtyard
5. Bon Hang Tuong Da — stone statues
6. Nha Bia — stelae house
7. Tru Bieu — epitaph
8. Ta Buu Truc Phong — left and right chambers
9. Dien Khai — entrance
10. Phong Dat Thi Hai — the catacomb
11. Phong Tho Vua — King's chamber
12. Nha — bep-kitchen
13. Nha Quan Cu — mandarins residence
14. Gieng Nuoc — well

probably be disappointed with the exterior appearance but this will certainly not be so when he enters the tomb proper at the top of the stairs. The jade colour of the walls and the ceilings of the left and right antechambers has been skilfully imitated. The huge 'Dragon in the Clouds' mural on the ceiling of the middle chamber is considered to be the largest and most ornate in Vietnam.

The mausoleum is also well known for its frescos — inlays covered with hundreds of thousands of colourful ceramic and glass fragments. The inlays depict trees, flowers, bamboo, animals and falling rain. This form of original bas-relief would delight the painter visiting the complex. It is a nightmare for the photographer because of all the reflective surfaces. Inside the mausoleum is a bronze-coloured life-size statue of King Khai Dinh.

The tomb of Gia Long

Few tourists will go to Gia Long's tomb because it is a long, difficult route — 14 km from Hue, and it is partly bomb damaged. The tomb was built in 1814, six years before his death.

The Minh Thanh temple in the grounds is dedicated to the emperor and his first wife Queen Thua Thien Cao. It was erected on Mount Bach. It is in a bad state of repair. To the left around the base of the Minh Thanh temple is Gia Long's sepulchre. At the very bottom is the funeral court. The Bai Dinh courtyard towered above the funeral court. Since becoming extensively damaged, the area is less popular but is still a very attractive place with Mount Thien Tho behind.

Other points of interest in Hue

The Thien Mu Pagoda   This is probably the only pagoda the tourist will have time to visit. It stands on the banks of the Perfume River. Formerly called Linh Mu, this seven storey Phuoc Duyen tower is 21 m high. It is said that the sound of the bell from the Thien Mu is familiar to countless generations of people. It is reached by tourist boat from the Perfume River Hotel. The Pagoda, which is Buddhist, was built in 1601 by Nguyen Hoang, the first governor of the southern court of Hue. It is believed that the bricks used in the construction are of Cham origin. Beyond the tower is the Buddhist sanctuary which is guarded by six genies. A glass case contains a gilded statue of the Laughing Buddha who represents happiness and prosperity. The inner enclosure contains three magnificent statues of Buddha enclosed in glass. The giant bell in the complex was cast in 1701.

Other pagodas   If time permits, visits to the other pagodas: Dieu De, Bao Quoc, Ngoc Tran, Tu Dam, Linh Quang and Tuong Van can be arranged by the Tourist Authority. It is just as easy to find them if you study the map in this book.

Dong Ba trading quarter The area which contains the main shops and stores.

Gia Hoi quarter Old houses.

Le Loi quarter The site of the old administrative centre of French times.

Nam Giao The altar to Heaven and Earth where the king used to officiate each year.

The Tiger Arena Here tigers were pitted against elephants in savage combat for the entertainment of the king.

Thuan An A beach on the coast.

Tourist Facilities — Hue
Hotels
The main tourist hotel in Hue was designed by one Ngo Viet Thu who also designed the Independence Palace in Ho Chi Minh.

Huong Giang (Perfume River Hotel) 52 Le Loi, Hue. Tel: 2122–2288. Price range: US$50 — 60

A very comfortable hotel with a gorgeous view of the Perfume River. Every one of its 42 rooms is air conditioned. The showers are a bit primitive and the beds a bit hard. The cuisine is superb, if anything you have too much to eat, and it's served by delectable women with names like Hung and Ha. Photographers should note that the receptionists at the Perfume River Hotel are available for hire, (for photos, that is) at US$5 per day. They will make your Imperial City tour and your visit to the Imperial tombs memorable.

The hotel has a large souvenir shop, a video room, table tennis, and laundry service. Royal dances are performed at the request of tourists, and the reception can arrange a visit to a *tuong* (classical opera). If you do not have Quy-Nhon on your programme, go to the tuong here (see the section on Quy-Nhon for the explanation of tuong).

Thuan Hoa Hotel. 78 Nguyen Tri Phuong, Hue. Tel: 2553, 2576.

Not nearly up to the class of the Huong Giang. Very few western tourists stay here — it is mainly for Russian delegations and Vietnamese tourists. Services include restaurant, bar and industry. Price range is US$20 — 30.

In Hue I think you should treat yourself, and if you are not on an international guided tour, request the Huong Giang as your hotel.

Other addresses
Tourist Office. 51 Le Loi Street, Hue. Tel: 2369.

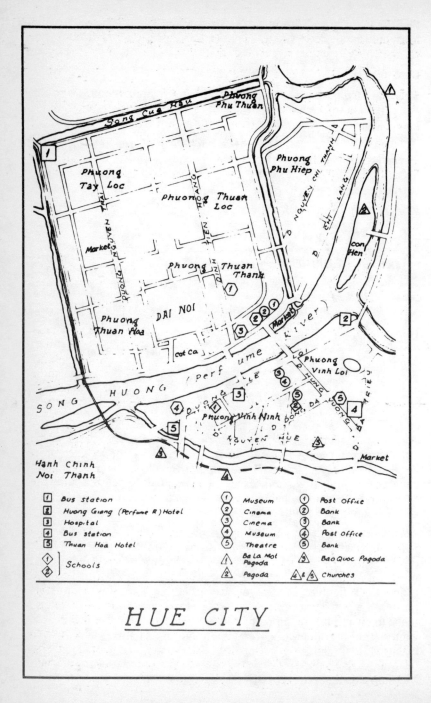

HUE CITY

Post Office The main one is 8 Hoang Hoa Tham. If you ask the receptionists at the Perfume River Hotel to post your mail, they will charge you way above the correct price.

Bank 6 Hoang Hoa Tham. Tel: 3699.

Theatres There are two: Hung Dao, on Duong Tran Hung Dao, which you can book through the reception at the Perfume River Hotel, but if I were you I'd go straight there and save money; Nha Hat Thanh Pho, which is the central theatre on Duong Hung Vuong.

There are three **cinemas** in central downtown Hue. These are the Dong Ba, Gia Hoi, and Hung Dao. A better bet is to use the video room in the Perfume River Hotel.

Hospital Emergency treatment can be obtained at the General Hospital, 16 Le Loi, Hue. Tel: 2325.

Excursions From Hue

The Tourist Authority will organise visits north into Binh Tri Thien province. Another two days should be allowed to see everything mentioned below.

T54 Tank ruins built by the Russians can still be seen on the roadside between Hai Lang and Quang Tri. These were damaged and later abandoned in 1972 at Ai Tu. The old church at Quang Tri is still left as a reminder of the war. The area was the site of extensive fighting during the battle of Con Tien. Piles of old 105 Howitzer shells can be seen at some of the poor residences on route. Recycling the metal from these still brings in a meagre income for the people of the area, although some farm areca nuts, tea, bananas and pineapples.

A maze of **underground tunnels** was built at Vinh Moc village, Binh Tri Thien province, in 1965, to cope with the US war of destruction. It consists of three tiers and measures 2,035 m. There were dozens of cubicles for living, and many large rooms for public meetings or for use as hospitals. Seventeen babies were born underground during the time of US bombings.

The Hien Luong (17th parallel bridge). This formed the dividing line between North and South Vietnam. It was closed from 1954 to 1975. It can be reached from Dong Ha, the site of an old US aircraft base just north of Quang Tri. The route goes via Con Thien which suffered tremendous fighting in the summer of 1967. This was a strategic position for work to begin on the McNamara defence line — a barrier to be built straight across the southern edge of the De-Militarized Zone. The barrier was to be strengthened by barbed wire and extensive mine fields on both sides. It was never completed. During the war, a five mile De-Militarized Zone between North and South Vietnam existed in theory only. Con Thien was two miles south of this zone, the bridge was in the centre. Those interested in the battles and operations undertaken in the area such as Hickory, Lamson, Buffalo, Beau Charger and Belt Tight should consult *Nam — The Vietnam Experience* series published by Orbis.

The American base at Khe Sanh

In my opinion this is not worth going to, but the road there takes the tourist along Route 9 which proved to be very important for the war effort. At Cam Lo, once the site of a small American base, Lao minority people can often be seen selling silk in the market. Some of the men of this minority have a Buddhist swastika tattoo on their wrists. This road served as one of the main arteries to supply Khe Sanh base and was used by the South Vietnamese army troops during the invasion of Laos in March 1971. As the visitor approaches Huong Hoa (Khe Sanh), the rolling green mountain scenery shows little evidence of the massive bombing which must have occurred during operation Niagara to protect the Khe Sanh base. The siege, which took place at Khe Sanh in January/February 1968 partly served as a diversionary tactic for the Tet offensive in the south. All that is left around the base is barbed wire, derelict buildings, parts of old trucks and cars and some shell castings.

The Bru Van Kieu minority

This part of Binh Tri Thien province is the area where you will find the 'Vil', or village of the Bru Van Kieu people. They still live very primitively, working the Ray or burnt out jungle area to grow rice. They can often be seen loaded up with sticks walking along Route 9 in the Khe Sanh area. It is relatively easy to visit their villages. They are not as shy as many minorities and love to be photographed. Their houses are built on stilts and are shaped in a tortoise shell fashion. Each house contains a room for the elderly, a room for belongings and a room for the couple and their children. The bark of the *xui* tree is used to make fibres for clothes and mats. It is not uncommon to see teeth coated with black lacquer. The family is very much male dominated.

The Ho Chi Minh Trail

Some of the smaller arteries can be visited with the help of an experienced guide. The Bru Van Kieu people are very familiar with the route of this trail in western parts of Binh Tri Thien province — during the war they helped to maintain it. They were very anti-American and had tremendous respect for Ho Chi Minh. Since the August Revolution (1945) all the Bru Van Kieus have adopted Ho as their first name.

The portions of the trail which still exist in this area are somewhat overgrown, but tourists will be suprised at the width of the trail and its good condition. The trail, aptly known as 'Hanoi's road to victory', was the idea of the North Vietnam Politburo. Even in 1959 existing pathways extended down from North Vietnam through Laos into Kampuchea (then Cambodia). Gangs of young men and women known as 'the Youth Shock Brigade' and many units of the Vietnam People's army were involved in its construction. They were given the code name Army Corps 559. The route served as a supply line for ammunition, food and medicine to the revolutionary forces in South Vietnam, Kampuchea and Laos. At the start, 500 men were divided into survey teams who examined the trails through the Truong Son Range of mountains. Thanks to the support of the local populations and strict secrecy, this system of roads was detected only after a very extensive web had been constructed.

The Americans sent out surveillance planes from the base at Dong Ha. Using sophisticated infra-red photography, they pin-pointed many campfires which at night showed up as white dots on this type of film. At first, everything on the trail was carried by individuals or on chainless bicycles, their handle-bars supported by long extension poles. In 1965 the first Soviet and Chinese-built trucks appeared on the trail. The total length of the system was 16,000 km and comprised five main roads, 21 branch roads and thousands of kilometres of detours. There were also 3,140 km of camouflaged roads. The defoliation mission of the C-123 planes which dropped Agent Orange, Blue, and White on the trail areas didn't succeed in showing up all the arteries. The North Vietnamese army were not even discouraged by the massive B-52 airstrikes in 1971 when millions of bombs came raining down on the trail. It was soon rebuilt and supplies continued to be moved. The invasion of Laos by the South Vietnamese army slowed down supplies to the South but due to the tenacity, resourcefulness and courage of the transporters an estimated 10,000 tons of supplies were getting through in late 1971. The Americans had realised how effective the trail was when the Tet offensive broke in 1968. During the 1973/1974 period specially equipped B-57 bombers sporting laser guiding systems scored lethal hits which disrupted movement along the trail. You should visit the trail inside the Vietnamese border if only to get an idea of difficulties that the builders must have had in this mosquito-infested malarial paradise.

Hue to Danang

It is invariably raining when travellers head for the Hai Van mountain range. This rises to around 6,000 feet above sea level and divides the Northern and Southern Trung Bo. Once through the Hai Van Pass the visitor is in the third natural region of the country. In the Southern Trung Bo the average temperature is said to be around 26°C. The high mountain barrier must play an important role in shielding the southern area from the chiefly northern winds.

From the Cul the lagoons of Cau Hai and Lang Co can be barely seen. Lang Co is a small oyster fishing village where courteous village folk will offer the visitor boiled oyster cooked on a mangrove charcoal fire.

Duck herder near Hai Van pass.

Guardian at Huyen Khong Cave, Danang.

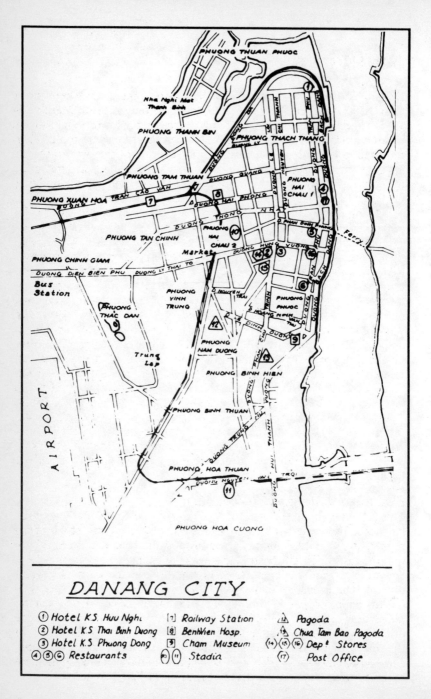

DANANG CITY

① Hotel K.S. Huu Nghi	⑺ Railway Station	⚐ Pagoda
② Hotel K.S. Thai Binh Duong	⑻ BenhVien Hosp.	⚐ Chua Tam Bao Pagoda
③ Hotel K.S. Phuong Dong	⑼ Cham Museum	⑭⑮⑯ Dep.t Stores
④⑤⑥ Restaurants	⑩⑪ Stadia	⑰ Post Office

DANANG

Danang is mostly remembered by the world as the place where more than 3,500 American marines first landed in the south on March 8th 1965. There have been a lot of changes since then, new trees have been planted along many streets, the parks are full of flowers, and life has returned to normal. The extent to which the authorities are striving to improve the tourist image can be seen by visiting Ham Bua park, once the site of massive rubbish dumps. Other visible signs are the building of the Chi Lang stadium and the Con market complex.

Danang, then called Cua Han, was once a small fishing village. Its other names have been Tourane (named in 1885) and later Thai Pien.

Don't fail to get up early in Danang and head for the Nguyen Van Troi bridge where thousands of bicycles can be seen streaming across to the factories in the suburbs. Since its days as a massive military base the city has changed immensely. Its inhabitants have proved to be resourceful and courageous but still remember that their province was one which suffered the heaviest material and human losses during the war. Materially, the city of Danang has been spared by the war, but on a social plane it was another story. The barbed wire is gone, new blocks of houses have sprung up, state-run and private stores supply all kinds of commodities delivered from Ho Chi Minh and Hanoi. Le Lion Street, Dien Bien Phu Avenue and Tran Phu now echo with the sounds of bicycle bells, thriving cafés, shops and handicraft centres. Tourists can purchase rugs, bamboo handicrafts, wood carvings and rattan. Those interested in wood carvings should ask the Tourist Authority to take them to the village of Kim Bong. If they want marble carvings, they can purchase these from the marble workshops at the base of the marble mountain.

Excursion to the Marble Mountain

This is the highlight of a visit to Danang. About 8 km from the city the landscape is dominated by Ngu Hanh, one of the five limestone peaks representing the five planets going around the sun. It was from here that the resistance fighters took pot-shots at enemy helicopters. A local legend says that the Ngu Hanh mountains are the eggs of a giant dragon. The range contains Mounts Thuy (water), Moc (wood), Tho (earth), Hoa (fire) and Kim (metal) — the five basic components of the universe. They were undoubtedly Cham centres of worship — ancient bricks have been found and Cham inscriptions in some of the caves. In the reign of King Le Thanh Ton (late 15th Century) the range became a famous beauty spot in Vietnam. The paths and roads linking them all together were constructed during the reign of King Minh Menh.

Many fierce battles took place on these mountains. Women gunners from Hoa Hai commune pounded the Nuoc Man airfield near Da Nang City. Many liberation fighters sacrificed their lives to defend statues and pagodas in the area.

Guides will show the tourists two trails which lead up the mountain. The devout can buy joss-sticks from small children en route. One trail leads up the southern side to the Tam Thai pagoda (156 steps) and the other on the eastern side to the Linh Ung pagoda (108 steps) — count them if you like! There are two observation posts Vong Giang and Vong Hai from where there is a magnificent view of the surrounding countryside. My guide told me that during the war the American military machine had wreaked havoc — the province had almost been turned into a desert. Now, from the view points, new filao forests can be seen, holding back the sand which continually blows inland from the Pacific. This sand had previously smothered the villages which were already war damaged.

The Tam Tai Temple

This was originally built in 1825 and rebuilt in 1946 and 1975. The central figure is the Buddha Sakya Mouni, below which is a small picture of Thich Ca. On the right is Quan Am, the goddess of mercy, and a statue of Van Thu symbolising intelligence, clairvoyance and wisdom. On the left is a statue of the boddisatva Quan Am and a statue of Pho Hien symbolising forgiveness, leniency and generosity.

Behind the temple is the Hoa Nghiem Cave which contains a statue of Quan Am. Before 1970 there had been a gilded Buddha statue but it had been stolen. Further on is the famous Huyen Khong Cave.

Explanation of who Quan Am was

Her other name is Thi Kinh. She was married to a student from a rich family. One night she attempted to remove a hair with scissors from her husband's chin while he was asleep. Waking up, thinking she was trying to kill him, he banished her from their house. She sought sanctuary in a temple and began a life of religious devotion disguised as a man. A young girl Thi Mau fell in love with Thi Kinh but was rebuked. Thi Mau became pregnant and named the monk Thi Kinh as the father. She was disgraced because everyone believed she was a man. The King of Heaven knew that this was a lie and sanctified her to be the Goddess of Mercy who brings love to every one. The container which she holds in her hand, Binh Cam Lo, contains magic water which protects people from hardship and distress.

The Huyen Khong Cave

This is an amazing Buddhist sanctuary. The best time to visit is between 11 am and 12 am when the light shining through the five holes in the 30 metre high roof lights up the central figure of Sakya Mouni (remember to take some fast film with you). The cave served as a guerrilla base during the Vietnam War. The Hoa Vang female guerrillas destroyed 19 American planes on April 15th, 1972. A sign in the cave also commemorates Phan Hanh Son who, on the 21st August 1963, helped in the destruction of 18 US planes.

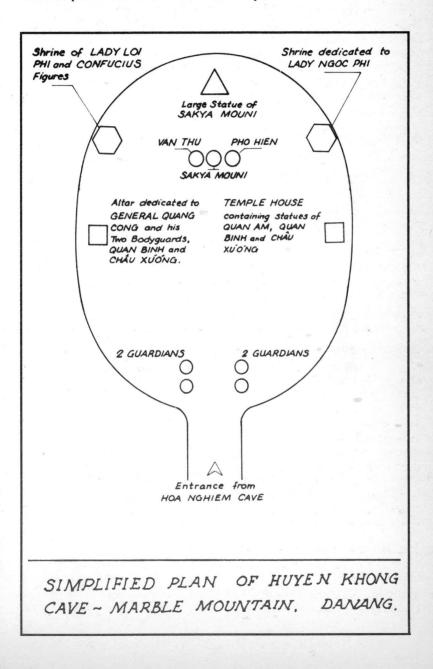

Shrine of LADY LOI PHI and CONFUCIUS Figures

Shrine dedicated to LADY NGOC PHI

Large Statue of SAKYA MOUNI

VAN THU   PHO HIEN

SAKYA MOUNI

Altar dedicated to GENERAL QUANG CONG and his Two Bodyguards, QUAN BINH and CHÂU XUỐNG.

TEMPLE HOUSE containing statues of QUAN AM, QUAN BINH and CHÂU XUỐNG

2 GUARDIANS   2 GUARDIANS

Entrance from HOA NGHIEM CAVE

SIMPLIFIED PLAN OF HUYEN KHONG CAVE - MARBLE MOUNTAIN. DANANG.

The Cham Museum

The museum of Cham sculpture is a must for any tourist itinerary. It contains sculptures from the 4th to the 14th Centuries. A small booklet can be obtained in Hanoi at the Foreign Languages Publishing House with details of the museum. It is difficult to obtain in Danang but occasionally they may have a copy at the Tourist Office — 48 Bach Dang Street — or the bookshop at 97 Phan Chu Trinh Street (Tel: 22760). It also has some interesting information on the Cham civilisation. However, books in English are notoriously difficult to get in Vietnam.

The open-sided museum is in a beautiful setting and contains 300 religious figures from Quang Nam, Binh Dinh and Quang Binh. The figures, mostly in sandstone, are exhibited in period rooms. The museum was started under the patronage of the École Française D'Extrême Orient in Hanoi. The statues, according to the area of origin and style, can be classified accordingly.

The Myson Room 4 (8th and 9th Century)   The statues show that Cham art was influenced by Indian and Khmer design. There are also faint hints of a Thai influence. The complex Myson was originally built by the King Bradravarman. He used to go to Myson after victory in a battle to pay homage to Hindu Gods — Vishnu and Shiva. It includes a variety of statues — Dan Sinh Than Brahma (Brahma, the God of Creation), Than Siva (Siva, the God of Destruction) and Than Ganesa (Ganesh, the God of Fortune) — his elephant head representing wisdom and luck, the snake around his body representing his innermost self. The Myson El altar is a masterpiece of Cham art depicting rituals of Hindu priests.

Tra Kieu Room   This contains carvings dating from the late 7th Century and the later Tra Kieu style up to the 10th Century. The early carvings show many animal styles and the wedding ceremony of Princess Sitra. Many heavenly maidens are depicted showing a definite Khmer influence. The later styles had undoubtedly been influenced by Indonesian art because of the relations between the northern Cham court and Java in the 10th Century. The most outstanding work in this style is a shrine worshipping beautiful dancing girls. The girls are carved in their Tribhanga position — with gracefully bent bodies.

The An My Room (early 8th Century)   This style features human statues with spiralling hair falling down, wide open eyes, long straight noses and thick lips.

Dong Duong Room (end of 9th to early 10th Century)   This room displays a variety of Buddhist statues. Carved scenes tell stories of Mahayana Buddhism. There are scenes about Queen Maya in the Lumbini garden when she gave birth to Prince Siddharta.

Than Siva – Thap mam style – Nghia Binh.

In the large altar there is a bronze statue of Lokesvara. The statues are strong evidence of the importance of Buddhism to the Chams during this period.

Khuong My Room   This is the period after the Dong Duong period in which the figures developed a Khmer influence but retained Dong Duong characteristics. The one prominent feature of this period is the complicated head dresses.

Chanh Lo Room (11th Century)   These statues were created when Vietnam was a very troubled nation. There was a distinct fading of the Indonesian influence and the figures became more characteristically Cham.

Thap Mam Room (12th–14th Century)   As well as there being many Angkor type statues, larger animal carvings similar to Tra Kieu appeared. Highly decorative patterns are used and the figures are very elegant looking.

Yang Mum Room (end of 14th Century to beginning of 15th Century)   Statues found in Gia Lai, Kon Tum province arranged in a triangular fashion with legs hidden — very uncharacteristic of Cham art.

Visiting Cham Ruins
The Cham people, sometimes known as the Chiem or Chiem Thanh, can still be seen in Vietnam today. Many live in the province of Nghia Binh, Phu Khanh and Thuan Hai. The last king of ancient Champa,

Cham ruins.

Po Phan Ri, died late in the 18th Century. At this time many Cham people left Vietnam for Cambodia. The Kingdom of the Chams, known as Champa, arose in the late 2nd Century AD and was composed of four main centres: Vijaya — Nghia Binh province;

Kauthara — Phu Khanh province; Panduranga — Thuan Hai province; Amaravati — from Binh Tri Thien to Quang Nam — Danang.

Tourists in Vietnam are very surprised at the extent of the former
Kingdom of Champa. Many visiting Danang will have to be content
with just seeing the Cham museum. The tourist who requires greater
insight into the Cham civilisation should make a request at least two
months before visiting the area and ask for a programme which would
give them at least four days in Danang (to see other things as well),
two days in Quy Nhon and two days in Nha-Trang. Visits that should
be requested in the Danang area are outlined later in this chapter.

Having made a visit to the Cham museum the tourist will be aware
that the Cham architecture and sculptural vestiges are related to the
Cham's religious life. The goddess Uroja (meaning woman's breast in
the Cham language) is worshipped in many temples. Specialists from
all over the world come to study the old Cham remains.

My Son Ruins
Located 28 km west of Tra Kieu in Duy Xuyen district, visitors must be
prepared for a long walk. Take plenty of bottled water and a picnic
lunch, and leave anything heavy, such as excess camera equipment,
behind. I think it should be pointed out that massive B52 bombing
raids in the area destroyed many architectural masterpieces. Don't be
disappointed — it's in a very tranquil setting and well worth a visit.
Under the dynasty of King Bhadravarman this was a devout religious
centre. According to archaeologists the sanctuary was named Srisanabhadresvara and was dedicated to the worship of God Shiva —
Bhadresvara. The temples which remain are indelible hallmarks of the
architectural genius of the Cham people. In all there are 15 towers left,
the most remarkable being the Chua tower which is 24 metres high.

It takes a whole day to visit My Son and an exhausting one at that!

Dong Duong
Built under King Indravarman II this is a huge complex 60 km south of
Danang. The Buddhist monastery in the area was named after
Laksmindra-Lokesvara. The visit to the Cham museum should remind
visitors that the Dong Duong style is strong in Cham Buddhist art
features. The area is mainly of interest to the archaeologist; the
ordinary tourist would find it rather uninspiring. There are architectural works including remains of shrines and monasteries surrounded
by a two kilometre perimeter. It is also possible to go to the temples
and towers of Chien-Dan, Bang-An and Khuong My. There are many
exhibits at the museum from these areas.

Tra Kieu
Tourists should be warned that the Cham ruins in this area no longer
exist. All you see on arriving in Duy Xuyen district on the basin of the
Thu Bon river is a series of old trenches. It does give you an idea of the

extent of these ruins. Providing that it has been requested, the Tourist Authority will arrange a trip to Duy Son 2 Cooperative. This cooperative is said to be one of the most dynamic in the country and is situated in an area which was the home of one of the earliest Catholic communities in Vietnam. The Kingdom of Champa had its captial there from the 7th to the 10th Century. It is interesting to see how the surrounding hills have recovered from bomb and shell damage and defoliation. Visitors are sometimes shown around by Luu Ban, now the President of the cooperative, who was imprisoned for his struggle against US occupation.

Tra My District

This can be combined with a visit to Tra Kieu in Duy Xuyen district. Very few tourists go to Tra My. This mountainous region, 130 km southwest of Danang, is well known for cinnamon production. It has been exported for centuries to be used as a medication, and in the perfume and confectionery industries. Much of it ends up in Hong Kong. Ethnologists should note that special permission is required to visit the Kor, Mnong and Sedang people in this area. The hamlets of these people are extremely difficult to get to. Many of these minorities still lead a nomadic life, practising slash and burn culture on hill slopes. Cinnamon trees have been planted by the minorities and marked with their own special brand. They return, sometimes even 10 years later, to harvest the crop.

The journey to Tra My passes through many areas ravaged by war. The road passes vegetation which shines a luxurious green, but in other areas where chemical poisons were used no grass will ever grow. In Duy Xuyen district the green mulberry trees and golden cocoons of the silkworm can once again be seen. The road towards the district town of Tra My is lined by many new houses and there is still a great deal of rebuilding activity. The market here is well worth a visit for photographers. Some of the villages in the area were rebuilt many times during the B52 bombing raids.

The Ancient Town of Hoian

Tourists with only a short programme in Danang will miss Hoian. This is a charming town of two-storeyed, tile roofed, wood framed residences built along narrow streets. It is only 25 km southeast of Danang on the Thu-Bon river, 3 km from the Cua Dai estuary. The town of Hai Pho, which lay slightly to the east of present Hoian, was moved to the present site of Hoian in the 15th Century. It was probably the oldest town in southeast Asia. During the time of French colonization Hoian was known as Fai Fo. By the middle of the 15th Century Chinese traders used Hoian as a base for voyages to other parts of southeast Asia. Many Chinese settled in the area after the overthrow of the Ming dynasty. This explains the unique Chinese architecture which is a remnant of the Qing dynasty.

The beginning of the 17th Century saw the arrival of the Japanese, Dutch, English, Portuguese and French traders which brought with them Christian missionaries. In 1624 Alexandre de Rhodes, a French priest, came to Hoian to spread the Christian religion among the Viet people.

Points of interest

Japanese Pagoda   This was built on a bridge in the 17th Century. The carved roof indicates the influence of Japanese architecture. The Pagoda was restored during the reigns of Gia Long, Ming Mang and Khai Dinh. Recent restoration work has been carried out by the Culture and Information Department of Danang. Legend has it that a large water monster created havoc in this area and that the bridge and its pagoda were built to exorcise the monster.

Fuc Kien Pagoda   Well worth a visit if only to see the statue of the Heavenly Lady which is somewhat peculiar, to say the least. She was believed to afford protection to the mariners on their dangerous voyages.

The Weaving Looms   At present there are more than 600 looms in operation in the town, producing four million metres of cloth and silk fabrics per year.

The Japanese pagoda at Hoian

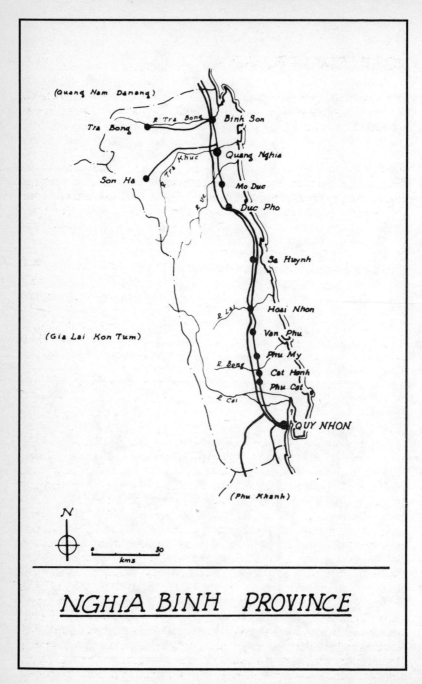

NGHIA BINH PROVINCE

NGHIA BINH PROVINCE

This resulted from the merger of the two former central Vietnam provinces of Quang-Ngai and Binh Dinh. Its northern boundary is marked by Mount Chuc, an offshoot of the Truong Son mountain range.

Climate

Because the Hai Van range of mountains in the north create a natural shield, the province is hot and humid. The dry season extends from March to May, and often it is very hot from May to July. The rainy season is from September to January.

Travelling through the province

Massive sugar plantations are seen around Binh Son. Very few visitors take the bumpy road to Tra Bong which was once a guerrilla base during the resistance periods against the French and Americans. The minorities in the area, Kinh, Hre, Bahnar and Kdong, helped to hide resistance fighters. The area is known for its prominent forests containing *Podocarpus*, *Hopea*, *Barian Kingwood* and bamboo which is made into wood pulp. The forests are rich in rattan, palm leaves, honey, medicinal herbs, resinous products and fungi.

From the Binh Son area you can drive for over 20 km until you reach the Cu Mong pass at the southern tip of the province. Approaching the town of Quang Nghia the visitor can, on a clear day, make out the granite peaks of Mount Ca Dam and Mount Da Vach. The dry period between March and July creates problems for the rice growers in this area, when the Tra Khuc river, which is crossed just before Quang Nhgia and the Ve river, which is crossed after this town, nearly run dry. Tourists should look out for the huge *norias* (12 m diameter irrigation wheels) which raise water from the river to the high paddy fields. This system has also helped the sugar cane plantations which supply huge quantities to the sugar refinery at Quang Nghia. As you leave this town, you pass a large cemetery which contains the bodies of two South Vietnamese battalions destroyed by the Vietcong. Alternatively, the tourist may like to head towards Son Ha in the Vach mountains to see cinnamon being grown. He will then pass through the famous Son Tinh district where a local guerrilla force had a resounding victory against the South Vietnamese army and US forces. The Ba Gia victory was followed by a massive invasion of US forces into the Binh Son area (where the traveller would have seen sugar cane plantations). Operation Starlight, as it was called, was aimed at destroying a large number of the invading Vietcong. The Van Tuong people, helped by guerrilla fighters and the Vietcong, gained a resounding victory against the 9,000 strong US Marines. The Vietcong marched into Quang Nghia on March 6 1975, and from here headed south towards Quy Nhon along the route which tourists take today.

Travelling between Quang Nghia and Quy Nhon

The road first crosses the Ve river and heads into the tobacco growing country of Moc Duc. The area is recovering from the 30 years of war against the French and US. During the war, many farmers had sought refuge in Quang Nghia, but after 1975 they went back to salvage what was left. A lot of the coconut plantations destroyed by the war and typhoons have been replanted. Sa Huynh is now a port big enough to take large ships. The salt marshes in the area are once more being fully utilised producing 60,000 tons of salt per year. The small hamlet of Tam Quan once again has stalls selling brushes and ropes made from coconut bristles. New plantations have sprung up in the Phu My Phu Cat area providing valuable copra oil used in margarine manufacture. At Phu My tobacco is being grown, and the Phu Cat military base is now used as an airport. You can head for Quy Nhon crossing the river Giao and divert to Thi Nai lagoon to see the large shrimp breeding station. Quy Nhon is now a large port accessible to 10,000 ton ships. During the war it was turned into an American base where Marines mingled with South Vietnamese, Australian, South Korean and New Zealand troops. It was a strategic position for launching attacks on the Central Highlands.

Tourist Facilities — Quy Nhon

Not many tourists arrive in Quy Nhon, from western countries. There is only one hotel on the seafront — ideal for an early morning swim if you don't mind sharing the beach with hundreds of small children!

Quy Nhon Tourist Hotel, 8 Nguyen Hue, Thanh Pho, Quy Nhon. Tel: 2401.

They have 40 rooms all air conditioned. 1st Class: 13 rooms at US$24 per night; Special Rooms: 24 at US$28 per night; 2nd Class: 25 rooms, US$17 per night.
The services include laundry, restaurant, souvenir shop, video and the occasional dance.

Restaurants: There is a restaurant in the tourist hotel but I would recommend eating in one of the small street restaurants in town and taking your own beer along.

When to Visit: The rainy season is September to February and the dry season March to August. The average temperature is 26°C.

Tourist Office: 4 Nguyen Hue, Thanh Pho, Quy Nhon.

Cinema: Le Loi Cinema, 20 Le Loi, Thanh Pho, Quy Nhon. Tel: 2815.

Usually Vietnamese or Russian films.

General Hospital: 102 Nguyen Hue, Thanh Pho, Quy Nhon. Tel: 2708.

Bank: 5 Le Thanh Ton, Thanh Pho, Quy Nhon. Tel: 2730.
No travellers cheques changed, only dollars cash.

Post Office: 127 Duong Hai Ba Trung, Thanh Pho, Quy Nhon. Tel: 2625.
The reception at the tourist hotel will post letters for you.

Tuong Theatre: 854 Nguyen Thai Hoc, Thanh Pho. Tel: 2804.
It's well worth going to see the Tuong.

Bookshop: 120 Duong Le Loi, Thanh Pho, Quy Nhon. Tel: 2509.

Evening entertainment in Quy Nhon

Enquire at the tourist hotel reception about Tuong. Classical opera was founded in this province by Dao Tan. It continued to be performed even through the war years. Whole families have devoted their lives to the opera. You may be lucky enough to met Uo Si Thua, the director of the Quy Nhon company who will explain the story of the performance through your interpreter. The performers make up with highly colourful face paints and wear eyecatching costumes. Every movement and expression has taken years to master.

Tay Son District

It is important that the visitor should know something about the history of Tay Son.

The formation of the Tay Son royal dynasty in the 18th Century was due to the Tay Son insurgency which was led by three brothers, Nguyen Nhac, Nguyen Hue, and Nguyen Lu. Visitors can now travel to Tay Son district in the Binh Dinh area where in 1771 the insurgency started. The base of the Tay Son uprising covers this area, as well as the greater part of An Khe district, Kontum province.

Visitors wanting to go to this historic site should take Highway Number One out of Quy Nhon, and then head west along Highway 19, 20 km from the capital. After around 35 km Tay Son (Phu Phong), capital of Binh Khe district, is reached. The upper Tay Son area, — the An Khe heights — are visible from here. This is the area where the three Tay Son brothers were born; the mountains in the area are named after them.

Your guide in Quy Nhon will no doubt tell you the story of the Tay Son era. Trouble between the Trinh lords in the north and the Nguyen in the south, had, in the 18th Century, brought ruin to the nation. The peasantry, who had been ruthlessly exploited, revolted. The Trinh and the Nguyen failed to put down the large-scale peasant uprisings. In 1771 the Tay Son brothers pursued a Robin Hood policy 'Take from the rich and give to the poor'. Nguyen Hue, who had amassed a huge peasant army, defeated the Trinh and the Nguyen troops, so putting an end to the division of the country. The Nguyen lords in the south rallied a massive Siamese army led by generals Chieu Tang and Chieu Suong with 20,000 men and 300 war junks. In 1784 Nguyen Hue left for Saigon with his troops and later arranged an ambush in the basin of the My Tho river between Rach Gam, and Xoai Mut. A Tay Son fleet of light warships lured the Siamese fleet, together with the Nguyen lord Nguyen Anh's army, into the trap. The Siamese army was defeated and Nguyen Anh's troops fled.

The victory of Rach Gam — Xoai Mut, which took place on January 20th 1785, not far from present day My Tho, had further consolidated national independence and laid the foundation for future victory over the Chinese. Nguyen Hue followed this up in January 1789 when he had a massive victory over the 200,000 strong Qing Chinese army which has been rallied by the Trinh lords in the north. He became a national hero; by defeating both the Siamese and Qing troops he had safeguarded national independence.

The Tay Son era ended after the death of Nguyen Hue in 1792, and the victorious battle in which Nguyen Anh, later to become the Emperor Gia Long, defeated his two brothers.

Festival

A good time to visit this area is the fifth day of the first lunar month when the Tay Son Festival takes place to celebrate Nguyen Hue's victory. The people in the district are very proud of this man who, at the age of 23, had defeated the Siamese and at 30, had defeated the Chinese. It is well remembered that on his return after the Sing victory he issued decrees to promote agriculture, encourage study, and lighten the tax burdens.

Today the festival is organised on the site of the Nguyen Hue (Quang Trung) museum. Tens of thousands of visitors make a pilgrimage to their hero's birth place. The lines of elephants and horses and the loud drum beats make the visitor think of Nguyen Hue's lightning attacks on the aggressors of Ngoc Hoi and Dong Da in the spring of 1789. Displays of martial arts are also given.

The Quang Trung Museum

A statue of Nguyen Hue stands outside the museum which was built in late 1977–1979 in Tay Son district. Inside there is another statue of Nguyen Hue and his two generals Ngo Thoi Nhiem and Ngo Van So. There are displays to remind the visitor of the Tay Son era. A memorial house dedicated to the Tay Son brothers which has been rebuilt in 1958 after being devastated during King Gia Long's reign, contains three altars. The one in the middle is dedicated to Nguyen Hue, on the left (facing) to Nguyen Lu, and on the right to Nguyen Nhac.

The Tet Festival

On the occasion of the Tet festival in the area, an exhibition of Tay Son martial arts is performed, Tay Son Vo Si. This includes the art of using weapons, on foot or on horseback, which was widely practised in Nguyen Hue's army. Nguyen Lu, his younger brother, devised a method by which men of small stature could defeat taller opponents. This he called the 'cock fight' method. It is believed that this form of martial arts originated from the Binh Dinh fighting school which only really suited strongly built men. The Tay Son Vo Si laid emphasis on flexibility. The champions of Vietnam live in the Phu Phong area.

Special arrangements

A special performance at any time can be arranged at the Nguyen Hue museum of Tay Son Vo Si. You must inform Vietnam Tourism of this request at least two months before coming to Vietnam if you are visiting Quy Nhon. It is well worth it — you may meet the grand master of this sport, Ha Trong Son, who, despite being in his seventies, can still give a dazzling performance.

Other visits in the area

An Luy Citadel   Not far from Phu Phong is the hamlet of An Khe. There are still remains of a citadel in this area which was believed to be a Tay Son stronghold. The heptagonal shape of the earthwork can still be seen. Two hills near the Mang Pass still bear the names of two insurgent leaders — Ong Binh (Nguyen Hue) and Ong Nhac (Nguyen Nhac) Hill. These are eight kilometres east of An Luy Citadel.

Hoang De (Imperial) Citadel   Its construction marked the first stage of development of the Tay Son movement. It was the site of a terrible battle between the Tay Son and Nguyen Anh's troops. It is now only a vestige — don't expect to see anything spectacular. Your guide will take you to the position, 27 km north of Quy Nhon, west of Highway Number One. National Highway One now runs through the northeastern part of the former city, and the railway through the northwestern and southern part. Many vestiges of Cham architecture, particularly the Mam Tower, are still seen inside the Hoang De fortified city. This capital, which was built by Nguyen Nhac, was once a bustling city — the ruins can still be seen over a large area.

Other Cham towers   Ask your guide to take you to the **Thap Doi** — twin Cham towers, which are being refurbished by UNESCO — and the **Duong Long** tower in Trung Dinh village, Tay Son district. You may also have time to visit the **Banh** tower in Tuy Phuoc district.

Other excursions from Quy Nhon
Leprosy village in Quy Hoa   How many tourists would like to go to a leprosy village I can't tell, but it's on the visitors' programme.

Cat Hanh village   People interested in the Vietnam War often request to go to Cat Hanh village near Phu Cat. In this village 80% of the houses were destroyed by American and Korean troops, and crops were devastated by toxic chemicals. Since the war it has been rebuilt and in 1979 received a UNESCO education award.

Journey from Quy Nhon to Nha Trang
This is a very scenic route particularly the Cu Mong Pass and the plains of Binh Dinh and Phu Yen. There are many picturesque bays where the traveller can stop to swim. During the bad typhoons of 1975 and the Vietnam war, many coconut plantations were damaged. These were replanted but again stunted by the drought in 1983.

The scenery along the winding roads changes from sugar cane plantations to tobacco fields and beyond, towards the long bridge of Tuy Hoa, rice.

Warning — no photography allowed in this area. This bridge is about 1 km long and one of the most famous in Vietnam. The Vietnamese authorities are tremendously sensitive about bridges. If a tourist is caught it will be his guide who is arrested and would probably lose his job!

A wonderful sight at sunrise are the numerous scoop nets on the Da river. New dykes and irrigation schemes have appeared since 1975. The rice fields have had most of their unexploded bombs removed but there are still accidents reported.

A cooperative visit   If you can request this in plenty of time (i.e. three months before going to Vietnam) you may be lucky. In 1987 the Hoa Thanh Tay cooperative managed to produce 18 tons of rice per hectare per year. This exceptionally high rate of production has only been beaten by Dai Phuoc cooperative in Quang Nam Da Nang province (20 tons per hectare per year).

Quy Nhon theatre: classical opera — Tuong.

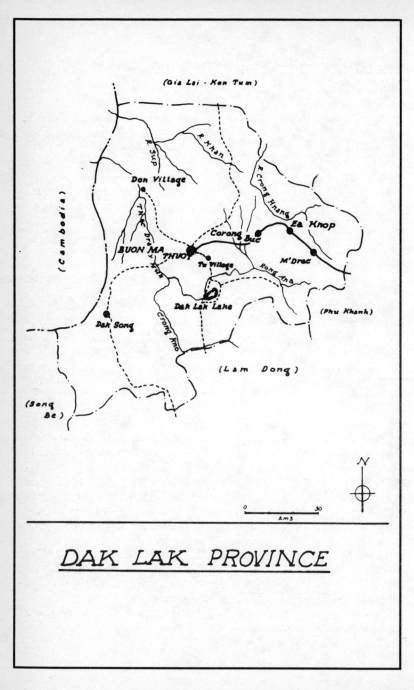

DAK LAK PROVINCE

TO BUON ME THUOT THROUGH DAK LAK PROVINCE

The best time to visit is outside the rainy season which is from April until November. They get the heaviest rainfall around August (321 mm). The temperature in the area is quite pleasant averaging 25°C, slightly hotter than at Dalat and definitely more humid all the year around.

Buon Me Thuot (Ban Me Thuot) is rarely visited by westerners. It isn't on any of the tourist programmes offered by Vietnam Tourism so to get there you must request it rather strongly. It is unlikely on your first visit to Vietnam that you will go to this area because of the hassle involved in getting through the stone wall bureaucracy that the authorities impose. If you insist on your second or third visit to the country, you just might make it. I have heard that the situation is getting rather more lax than this suggests, so best of luck!

This town in Dak Lak (Dac Lac) Province is situated to the southwest of the Truong Son range of mountains. The road (Highway 14) which branches off Highway Number One, north of Nha Trang, winds its way through the mountains zig-zagging as it goes. The heavy rain in the area has damaged it badly in places and it is quite a bumpy ride, although four wheel drive is not necessary. The Ede people can be seen working on the red basaltic soil which yields crops of rubber, coffee, tea, pepper, and a variety of orchard fruits. In the hollows, the minorities grow rice which is naturally well-watered at this elevation. The long houses of the Ede can barely be seen through the misty atmosphere of the mountain passes. The province has a big network of rivers; some flowing westwards empty into the Mekong via the Ea Krong, Ea Hleo and Serepok. A war statue at Ea Nop district reminds travellers that this was once not a peaceful place. The war monument in the centre of the capital Buon Me Thuot is unique; on a sloping pedestal stands the first Russian tank involved in the liberation of this town.

Readers interested in the war effort in the area should read *From Pleime to Buon Me Thuot* by Senior Lieutenant General Hoang Minh Thac. He describes the devastation released on the town during the attack by three North Vietnamese divisions.

You will have a fantastic time if you can get there, the people are extremely warm-hearted and outgoing.

Tourist Facilities — Buon Me Thuot

Hotels

Hotel Thang Loi: 1 Phan Chu Trinh. Tel: 2322.
This is the main tourist hotel used in this region. It is very basic, has a small restaurant and bar that the locals use. The food is adequate but not luxurious. It is one of the most friendly hotels in Vietnam.

Hong Kong Hotel: 30 Hai Ba Trung.

Hoang Gia Hotel: 2 Le Hong Phong.
These are used mostly by Vietnamese tourists.

Other addresses

Bank: On Duong Ama Tranglon. Take American dollars cash.

General Hospital: On Duong Nguyen Du.

Tourist Office: Dak Lak Tourist Office, 3 Phan Chu Trinh, Buon Me Thuot. Tel: 2322.
Ask for Duc — he'll arrange anything for you.

Museum

Situated just over the road from the Hotel Thang Loi, at 1 Me Mai, with a lovely guide, Mrs Bui Kim Nga. Tourists should find the place fascinating, especially if they are interested in ethnic minorities. There are 31 ethnic groups in Dak Lak province, the majority being the Ede, M'nong and Giarai, and in the minority the Muong, Thai, Dao, Tay and many others which are less common.

The museum features some pictures of the minorities in their traditional costumes, and displays of objects in everyday use. These include hats, shields, farming tools, fishing tackle, rice threshing devices, bows and arrows, weaving frames, and sets of musical instruments. Those of the Ede people are very peculiar. There is a drum made out of bamboo, tubes of different sizes making the sound vary, with a water buffalo skin, *dan trung*, and many different types of gongs. There is even a model of an Ede house. This is similar to the long houses seen in Iban territory in Sarawak. The house has a thatch roof, and is supported by wooden poles. Inside it is divided into sections, each accommodating a family. If the person is fairly wealthy they have two ladders at the house entrance. The largest one is used for honoured guests and is decorated with carvings in the shape of the moon, stars and a woman's breasts. There are also intricate carvings of turtles and lizards on the house.

Interesting visits outside Buon Me Thuot

Duc at the tourist office will arrange for tourists to visit the local minorities. Note, however, that if you are an ethnologist you should have requested a visit to these minorities many months before visiting Vietnam. Special permission has to be arranged through the authorities in Ho Chi Minh and Hanoi. It must be emphasised again that it is extremely difficult to get Buon Me Thuot included in your programme. The area is visited mostly by foreign coffee delegations, Russian and Cubans, Duk knows the chiefs of Tua village (Ede minority) and Don village (mostly M'nong minority but also Ede, Giarai, Lao, Khmer, Thai, Bahnar and Viet). He can't take you there unless he has had permission from the authorities first.

Tua Village (13 km from Buon Me Thuot)
This is a very friendly Ede stronghold. You should take them some salt, cigarettes and candies for the children. It has a population of 308, in 47 families. The traditional thatched roofs have gone, now replaced by tin sheeting. The people make a living from farming, mainly growing sweet potatoes, manioc, and maize and breeding livestock and weaving cloth. You may be lucky enough to visit the local school. Poor families have shorter houses, rich ones have a long house or Sang Dok which is 50 to 60 metres long with elaborate ladders (see description in *Museum*). The chief told us that the Ede people call themselves A-Nak-De which is either the name of a kind of bamboo forest where these people used to live, or it comes from the name of the supreme God of the tribe. Many of the families in the village have descendants from other Ede sub groups the Kpa, Athan, Krung, and Mthur.

Don Village
Forty five kilometres from Buon Me Thuot is Don village in Ea Sup district, home of a mixture of minority people but predominantly M'nong. We are told by Masen, the chief, that it wasn't long ago that there was fierce fighting between the M'nong and the Ede. Today they live in peace. The M'nong are elephant hunters and Don village has 56 domesticated elephants which are used in wild elephant hunts. The villagers have to grow massive amounts of sugar cane and grass to feed these animals.

In a nearby village, Krong Ana, there is a white elephant about five years old captured by a well known elephant hunter, Mr Ama De. It is the third white elephant to be captured in the Ea Sup district. The second one was confiscated by President Ngo Dinh Diem and sent to the United States in the 1960s.

It is believed, from archaeological evidence, that elephants were first domesticated in Vietnam during the Dong Dau period, about 3,000 years ago. They were used in the storming of the Co Loa Citadel and by the Chinese invaders, and against the Chinese during the Trung sisters uprising in 248 AD. During the Tay Son uprising they were used extensively and, in the Nguyen dynasty, they organised fights between them and tigers in a special arena in Hue. Some of the elephants from Dak Lak province now end up in western zoos. They fetch over 1,000,000 dong each for the M'nong people. On the occasion of the 10th anniversary of its liberation (March 1975–1985) an elephant parade was held in Buon Me Thuot. The parade involved 33 big elephants carrying beautiful howdahs marching 11 abreast in rows of three, with three young elephants accompanying their mothers.

The chief, deputy chief and elders invite foreigners to partake of rice wine, drunk out of a Che container. This is performed in the traditional way with everyone sitting in a circle around the large, ceramic pot and drinking the ferment through long bamboo straws. Visitors have been invited to ride around the district in the company of the chief on the back of an elephant. On rare occasions a musical performance using a set of six different sized gongs is given. These have very lyrical names, Khah, Lhiang, Mdu Khok, Hlue Khok, Hlue Lhiang, and Hlue Khok Diet. Another set of three gongs, Ana-Ching, Mdu-Ching and Mong Ching accompany the drummer who plays the Ngor. After a few rice wines it is not long before everyone is dancing.

The performers unfortunately now wear western type dress but a few members of the community do wear the *Myeng Lang* (women's skirt) and the *Kpin* (male wrap-around). The men wear several bracelets, one is often given to the visitor as a sign of friendship. The visitor is often invited to chew the betel nut and smoke tobacco.

Other Minorities in Dak Lak Province

Ethnologists should see the book written on *The people of Dak Lak province* by Be Viet Dang, Chu Thai Son, Vu Thi Hong. It was published by the Social Science Publishing House in Hanoi in 1982. You must be able to read Vietnamese. Mentioned in the book are the Ede people in the northeast and northwest of the province. Important information on the Xodang, Bahnar and Giarai is included. Many ethnologists visiting Vietnam find it extremely difficult to get this type of information. Enquire at the Institute of Social Sciences, 38 Hang Chuoi Street, Hanoi. Tel: 52345.

Coffee Plantations

Request a visit to a coffee plantation at the tourist office. The plantations were flattened during the Vietnam war but have now recovered considerably. The reason is probably because the species of *Robusta* grown is very hardy and can become productive after four or five years. The best coffee cooperative to visit is Doan Ket. This cooperative grows its crops on land previously used for a bamboo forest. It has built an extensive irrigation system and its productivity is so high that Russian coffee experts visit it to gain some tips. Mr Pham Van Thu (who shows you around) is very proud of the cooperative's achievements. If you are lucky you will also be treated to a visit to the processing factory where the coffee is dried, ground, sorted, sifted and packed for export to East Germany, Soviet Union, Japan and Hong Kong.

Lak Lake: Here you can see the summer house of Bao Dai.

Drai Sap Waterfall: An interesting journey through the rainforest where you will see black wood, iron wood and teak. The waterfall is about 12 km from Buon Me Thuot. During the rainy season you will get soaked by the spray.

KONTUM PROVINCE

Few tourists travel through this province. It can be reached from Highway Number One from Buon Me Thuot. Huong Huu is a Cotu minority settlement which is rarely visited by westerners because the Tourist Authority do not encourage use of the highway which leads eventually to Buon Me Thuot in Dak Lak province. The Cotu have taken up wet rice cultivation in the Nam Dong valley. Many dams, reservoirs and irrigation channels have been built. They also grow bamboo, pineapples and bananas and raise livestock. There are many minorities in the province including Bahnar, Sedang, Gie-Trieng, Brau, Ro Mam and Gia Rai. After liberation many of the tribes suffered dreadful hunger. The revolutionary administration, through educational schemes, taught land reclamation programmes, the building of reservoirs and irrigation channels, and set up large cooperatives which, through collectivisation, improved their crop yields immensely. It was a difficult job to teach some of the tribes to become sedentary farmers but now, thanks to state organisation, 90 cooperatives and 1,000 or more production collectives have been set up. The rich red basaltic soil of the province has been used to grow tea, rubber, cotton, coffee, sesame, beans and ground nuts. Grasslands have been used to improve cattle stocks and forests are being exploited for their timber and medicinal products. In 1986, 900 medicinal species yielded 2,000–3,000 tons of medical substances, the most valuable of which were cinchona, cinnamon, and ginseng. The bamboo forests have been used for house building, and paper manufacture, *Pinus khasya* for resin and paper production. The *Khop* plantations have been carefully preserved because of their water retaining qualities while Trac, Mun, Gu Cam, Lim and Tau have proved to be useful for carpentry. The whole area is a haven for wild flying squirrels, peacocks, pheasant and in the south for wild elephants. The area is not yet open to tourism but there are rumours that a tourist department will soon be set up.

NHA TRANG — PHU KHANH PROVINCE

The best time to visit Nha Trang is the dry season from April to November. The splendid sandy beach at Nha Trang makes it a favourite spot for holiday makers. Along the sea front beyond the New Pasteur Institute one can drive to the fishing village of Cua Be about 10 km away. Few visitors arrive here and immediately they do, throngs of

NHA TRANG

small children cry out 'Lien Xo, Lien Xo!' (Russian, Russian). The fishing fleet return here every morning and much of the catch ends up in the Xom-Con fishing market overlooking the Cai river. Over the road from here is the very famous Cham temple area dating back to 817. The Cham towers are made of bricks, with no cement in between. The temple receives the full light of the midday sun. Inside the main tower is the Ponagar statue which was decapitated under French rule

— the head is now in the Gizée museum in Paris. A new head was moulded in Nha Trang. Ponagar was an early gynaecologist. Pilgrims visit the site every first and fifteenth day of the lunar month. During the Merian festival on the 23rd March and the 23rd October, Buddhists travel long distances to worhip Ponagar.

Longson Pagoda
From the rear of the Cham towers a magnificent panoramic view of Nha Trang can be seen. A prominent feature of the landscape is the huge, white Buddha of Longson Pagoda facing towards the east. This structure was built in 1963 to commemorate the successful struggle against the Diem regime. Under the foot of the statue are the images of nuns and monks who burned themselves as a final protest against Diem. The Buddha is 23 metres high, one million bags of cement being used in its construction. In the Longson Pagoda below, the monk Thich-Quang-Duc lived before his final protest when he burned himself in Ho Chi Minh (Saigon).

Other points of interest
An amazing spectacle in Nha Trang can be seen by standing on the Xom Bong bridge over the Cai river and watching the fishing fleet in the setting sun. During the day Cho Dam — main market — bustles with activity selling everything from vegetables and fruits to bicycles and toys made out of recycled aircraft parts. Some good handicraft shops are seen along Unification Street. The Oceanography Institute with over 60,000 species is well worth a visit. Also in Nha Trang is the Tri Nguyen aquarium. Other attractions which are a little out of the way are Truong Xuan hot spring (55 km), Dai Lanh beach (86 km), Ba Ho waterfall (30 km) and Doc Let beach (60 km).

Tourist Facilities – Nha Trang
Hotels

Hai Yen Hotel, 40 Tran Phu, Thanh Pho, Nha Trang. Tel: 22974 or 22828
   This is the biggest hotel with 104 air-conditioned rooms. The most expensive rooms are US$33 per day. There are 36 rooms at US$24 per day and 63 rooms at US$20 per day.
   Services include restaurant, barber shop, laundry, video, and dancing twice a week.

Thang Loi Hotel: 4 Pasteur, Thanh Pho, Nha Trang. Tel: 22241
There are 56 air-conditioned rooms at US$22 per day, services are the same as above.

Thong Nhat Hotel: 18 Duong Thong Nhat, Thanh Pho, Nha Trang. Tel: 22966

This is normally for Vietnamese tourists. Only 9 rooms are air-conditioned and services include laundry and restaurant.

Other addresses

Tourist Office: Phu Khanh Tourism, Tran Hung Dao, Thanh Pho, Nha Trang. Tel: 22753 or 22754

Bank: Foreign Trade Bank, 17 Duong Quang Trung, Thanh Pho, Nha Trang. Tel: 20154

Hospital: 1 Yer Sin, Thanh Pho, Nha Trang. Tel: 22168

Post Office: Duong Pasteur, Thanh Pho, Nha Trang. Tel: 10

Bookshop: 73 Duong Thong Nhat, Thanh Pho, Nha Trang. Tel: 22637

Theatres: Tan Tan, Duong Thong Nhat, Thanh Pho, Nha Trang.

Tan Quang, Duong Quang Trung, Thanh Pho, Nha Trang.

Cinema: Duong Hoang Van Thu, Thanh Pho, Nha Trang.

Xom Con fish market, Nha Trang.

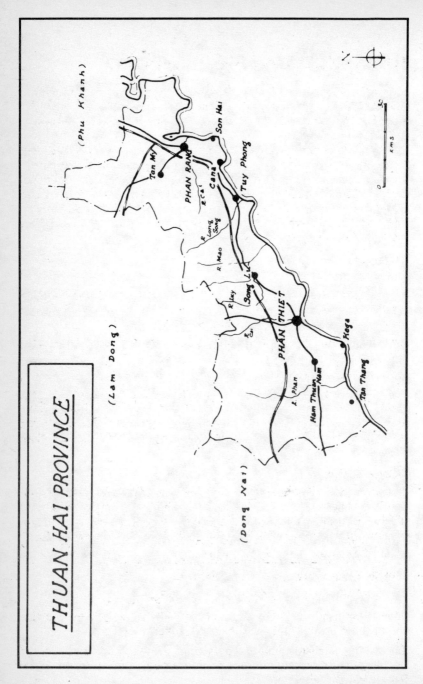

THUAN HAI PROVINCE

THROUGH THUAN HAI PROVINCE

Soon after leaving Nha Trang the coast road passes the deep natural bay of Cam Ranh, once an American Fleet stronghold.
Warning: no photography is allowed in this area which is now a Russian military base.

Near **Phan Rang** there are two old Cham towers now badly decayed. Some ethnologists like to stay in this area because of the colourful Cham people, who live in the foothills. If you want to visit traditional Cham residences you must get permission from the authorities. Deep in the foothill areas the Cham houses still have distinct buffalo horn frontages. They stage the Kate festival at the beginning of December but so far no westerner has attended it.

Hotels in Phan Rang
The hotels are extremely basic and the food simple.

Thong Nhat Hotel, Duong Thong Nhat, Thi Xa, Phan Rang, Thuan Hai. Tel: 2049
They have a restaurant and a souvenir shop.

Huu Nghi Hotel, Duong Huu Nghi, Thi Xa, Phan Rang, Thuan Hai. Tel: 74.

Ninh Chu Hotel. Tel: 2042
The best situated because it is on the beach. Visitors can also visit the Hang Temple in the town. Foreigners don't often stay at Phan Rang and the hotels are usually full of Vietnamese tourists. The hotels can be booked from Ho Chi Minh at the Thuan Hai tourist office, tel: Phan Rang 2475.

Phan Thiet
This is reached by travelling through very unfertile sand-covered land. Tourists come to Phan Thiet to visit the memorial complex dedicated to Ho Chi Minh. You can see the primary school that he once taught in, now known as the Duc Thanh School. Other attractions include:

Vinh Thuy beach, suitable for swimming.

Mui Ne beach, 3 km from Phan Thiet.

Ta Cu mountain, where there is beautiful scenery.

Nuoc Mam: fish brine factories. You should be warned that if you visit one of these establishments, the smell is overpowering.

The fishing harbour and the unloading of the catch early in the morning. This is a real bonus for photographers — over 100 species of fish are caught in this area!

Hotels
Tourist Hotel, 40 Tran Hung Dao, Thi Xa, Phan Thiet. Tel: 2574 or 2901.
There are 14 rooms, 7 first class at 1870 dong per night, and seven second class at 1210 dong per night. The services include restaurant, laundry, barber shop, video and souvenir shop. But I don't recommend this hotel — it's very dirty!

Vinh Thuy, Duong Nguyen Tat Thanh, Thi Xa, Phan Thiet. Tel: 2622–2655.
There are 38 rooms, the best one 5500 dong per night. It is a good place to swim in the sea. The restaurant is very good, and this is the best hotel.

Other addresses
Hospital: Duong Hai Thuong Lan Ong, Thi Xa, Phan Thiet. Tel: 2647.

Theatre: Nhan Dan, Duong Nguyen Tat Thanh, Thi Xa, Phan Thiet.

Bookshop: Duong Nguyen Hue, Thi Xa, Phan Thiet. Tel: 2757.

Post Office: Duong Tran Phu, Thi Xa, Phan Thiet. Tel: 2729.

Bank: Duong Tran Hung Dao, Thi Xa, Phan Thiet. Tel: 2626.

Other Points of Tourist Interest in Thuan Hai Province

Scenery
Thuan Hai, lying at the crossroads which connect north-south of Vietnam with Lang-Biang highlands, is an area rich in scenery. The famous scenic landmarks are the Belle-Vue Pass, the pile-up stone-hills, the swampland Lam Nai, the Tri Thuy mountain park, the Mui Le sand dunes, and the numerous sandy beaches Ninh Chu and Vinh Thuy.

Historical Sites
Poklong Garai and the Porome Temple, mausoleums which hold unique historical treasures of champa art. There are other historical landmarks, reminders of the French and American wars, there are Le Hong Phong Maquis, the triangle zone, the Ck7 Maquis, the Ca Du mountain site and the stronghold bases of Bac Ai, Anh Dung, Nam Son and Nam Thanh.

Industrial Sites
It is highly unlikely that the tourist would want to see the Da Nhim hydro-electric station or the Phuong Hai cement works. Many have, however, requested to see the salt mining at Ca Na, for which the area is ideally suited because of the long periods of drought when evapora-

tion is high from the salt marshes. Today Ca Na exports between 50,000 and 100,000 tons of salt annually. Most of the workers come from Lac Nghiep and Thuong Diem hamlets where their families have been salt producers for three generations. These are extremely tough individuals having to work daily in the open air at temperatures near 40°C.

THROUGH DONG NAI PROVINCE

Dong Nai province is made up of Bien Hoa, Long Khanh, and Ba Ria with an area of 7,588 square kilometres and 1.6 million inhabitants. The scenery varies tremendously, there are large rivers, long white sandy beaches, imposing mountains and forests, bazan soil for raffia plantations, and rubber trees, alluvial soil for rice, virgin jungle (*cat tien*), waterfalls, lakes and grapefruit-growing villages.

It contains the Bien Hoa industrial complex, together with the Tri An hydro-electric station and the Tuy Ha oil-chemistry factory.

Very old ceramics have been found in the province together with a xylophone dating back 3,000 years. During the insurrections against the French and Americans, the province is remembered for its staunch resistance zones, Minh Dam, La Nga and Xuan Loc.

Visits can be arranged by the Tourist Authority to: **raffia plantations**, which are very attractive, the glowing yellow strands are dried on the side of the road before being used for making roofs, hats, mats and baskets; **rubber plantations**, where demonstrations will be given of latex collection. The trees are generally over 50 years old and were originally planted by the French. If you are lucky you may get to see a rubber factory where the latex is treated with acetic acid which coagulates it before it is passed for flattening through rolling mills.

The roads through this province could do with some maintenance work, there are large pot holes in places.

Many local markets selling sweet potatoes line the road to Vung Tau.

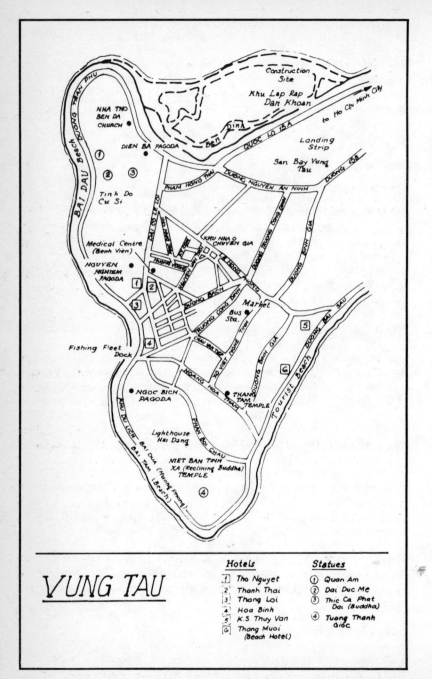

VUNG TAU

Hotels

1. Tho Nguyet
2. Thanh Thai
3. Thang Loi
4. Hoa Binh
5. K.S Thuy Van
6. Thang Muoi
   (Beach Hotel)

Statues

1. Quan Am
2. Dai Duc Me
3. Thic Ca Phat
   Dai (Buddha)
4. Tuong Thanh
   Gioc

VUNG TAU

This is a small peninsula 125 km east of Ho Chi Minh City. It is an important seaside resort, sunny all the year. There are numerous beaches to choose from: –

Thuy Van: 8 km long, clear water, fine sand.

Tam Duong: a small cove.

Bai Dau: very quiet, good for privacy.

Bai Dua: a string of smaller beaches within reach of hotels and villas.

A good panoramic view of the area can be obtained from Nghinh Phong mountain. The seaside resort was known as Cap St. Jacques in French times. Vietnamese tourists from Ho Chi Minh often come to Vung Tau for their holidays. During the war it was very popular with Australian soldiers. Now it has a large Russian petro-chemical industry which in no way interferes with the beauty of the area.

Points of tourist interest in Vung Tau

Ben Da fishing village   This is full of smiling children who cry 'Lien Xo, Lien Xo!', (Russian, Russian!). The locals are friendly enough and you can pass an interesting hour watching fish being skinned, dried and salted.

Bai Dau village   Here fishermen collect in their nets propelling their boats along by 'leg rowing'. They are not very friendly and it's difficult to get a decent photograph.

Villa Blanche   This was used by the last King of the Nguyen dynasty, Ba O Dai and later by Thieu, President of South Vietnam from 1963–1975. It is a good place to take snaps and to get a magnificent view of Vung Tau.

The Nirvana Meditation Temple   This is just around the corner from the main hotel region. It contains a reclining Buddha and is typical of Hinayana Buddhism. In the temple grounds there are many shell sellers.

Sakya Mouni Temple   *See map.*

Con Dao   This is a cluster of 14 islands, 50 minutes by plane from Vung Tau. It is a national park where many beautiful corals can be seen. The islands have lovely beaches with coconut palms. You can even visit the island where the *salanganes* birds nest in caves and watch the local nest collectors at work. Their nests are greatly valued by gourmets as a highly nutritious food. A new breeding centre for grey shrimps was opened in 1967.

Tourist Facilities — Vung Tau

Hotels

Although only a very small place, there are many hotels. The only hotel used by westerners is: –

Hoa Binh, just off Quang Trung Street. Tel: 2265, Telex: 307.

This has seven single rooms and 138 double rooms. The facilities include bar, shop, steam bath — massage, conference room and dance hall.

They will change money and post your letters at the reception. The restaurant is superb, specialising in every type of sea food imaginable. When this is full up, foreign tourists are accommodated at the Tam Thang, Thien Thai, Hanh Phuoc, and Thang Muoi which is near the beach.

If you are making your own way from Ho Chi Minh city and you want cheap accommodation, stay at the hotels the Russian oil experts use: Thang Loi, Song Hong, Song Huong or Tho Nguyet (see map for some hotel locations).

Cleaning the nets in the fishing village of Vung Tau.

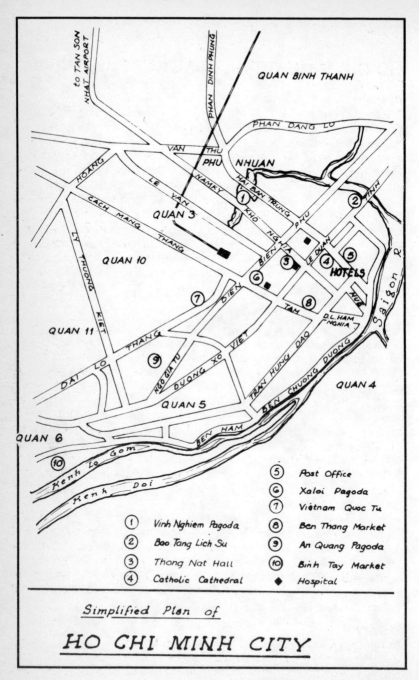

Simplified Plan of

HO CHI MINH CITY

Legend:
1. Vinh Nghiem Pagoda
2. Bao Tang Lich Su
3. Thong Nat Hall
4. Catholic Cathedral
5. Post Office
6. Xaloi Pagoda
7. Vietnam Quoc Tu
8. Ben Thang Market
9. An Quang Pagoda
10. Binh Tay Market
◆ Hospital

HO CHI MINH CITY (FORMERLY SAIGON)

Arriving
These days there are various ways of getting there. The most comfortable is via the sleek-bodied jets of Air France which take only one hour from Bangkok. The less fortunate may fly in on the Illyushin –18 turboprops of Air Vietnam. The most exciting is to travel down the old mandarin route on Highway Number One from the North. If you enter Vietnam via Tan Son Nhut airport, you can't help noticing beyond the paddy fields old rusting Huey helicopters, the remains of American fighters and B52 bombers. Don't be daunted by the huge concrete hangars and the antiblast wall which haven't been removed. The form filling (see page 22) is no longer a huge hassle, the building is now air conditioned, and the searches are far less vigilant. Photographers carrying too much film needn't worry, they don't even count them these days, and if they did, they wouldn't be put off if you have 200 rolls.

Getting to the city
Vietnam Tourism provide Japanese microbuses or, for the privileged, chauffeur driven cars with an interpreter. If you arrive unexpectedly, taxis are available at about 5,000 dong to the centre of the city. Why not catch the local bus for about 200 dong — few westerners would dare! Many foreigners entering Vietnam for the first time are absolutely paranoid from tales, often greatly exaggerated, appearing in the western press. In Ho Chi Minh these days there is virtually no security problem, and the authorities are far more lax about allowing foreigners to make their own way around. It is a different matter, however, when you try to travel around the country. Unescorted visitors should see the section on hotels in Ho Chi Minh for ideas about obtaining accommodation.

When travelling into the city, look out for the old sign on the underpass with the letters MACV — Military Assistance Command Vietnam. You won't see much motorised traffic although small motor bikes are appearing in great numbers since 1988. Along tree-lined wide boulevards, through the bustle of the bicycle jams, you will soon be at your hotel. If you are a journalist, don't head for the old Continental Palace because it's closed.

History
In the 15th Century, this area was only visited by wild beasts. During the 17th Century the land of the Nguyen lords was in lower Cochinchina. It was then a trade centre on the banks of a river and was

christened Dong Na. In 1698 it became a district of the Prefecture of Gia Dinh. Many consider that this is the birthday of the city, then called Ben Nghe (landing stage of the buffaloes), on the banks of a river infested with crocodiles which sounded like buffaloes). It has also been called Ben Thanh and today in Ho Chi Minh there is a market by this name. During the Tay Son era, it was selected as the capital of old Cochinchina and formed the site of many battles during the period 1777–1785. The capital was called Saigon by Le Quy Don in the 1728–1785 period. It became an important hub of communications after the building of the mandarin route to Hue in 1748 and the road to neighbouring Cambodia much later.

After Gia Long's and Ming Mang's reign in 1859, it was seized by the French. It was opened as a port one year later. The people have retained their courage, stamina and big-heartedness through years of struggle against foreign aggressors. The words of patriots who fought with swords and pen and ink still echo in the hearts of the people. In August 1945 there were great celebrations in Saigon as the revolution triumphed. This was only to last for 29 days. Since then many people have died. To many, Saigon is still remembered as the Pearl of the Orient, but to others it saddens their hearts.

Getting around Ho Chi Minh
By far the best way is to hire a rickshaw-like contraption called a cyclo. Many of the drivers know the city very well; they may tell you in broken English that they were once part of Diem's forces. Many will have real sob tales — who knows if it is just an attempt to get some more dong, dollars or cigarettes? Don't be too put off by the footless beggars and teams of small children repeatedly demanding money, just try to help them a little if you can afford it. Ask your driver to take you on the following route.

A good route around Ho Chi Minh by Cyclo
A good place to start is at the Doc Lap Hotel. Look out for a cyclo driver called Binh, he speaks good English. Try it at 6 o'clock in the morning before it gets too hot. Head down towards the river Saigon along Dong Khoi street, remembered as the area where the 'girlie' bars used to be during the war. Your cyclo driver may try to entice you to go back later and do some shopping in the handicraft stores where he gets commission. In the Nha Rong wharf area you will see many people shadow boxing opposite the old Majestic Hotel. If you take a short walk here you will undoubtedly be approached by people asking for soap or shampoo — it's expensive in Vietnam. You can visit the Ho Chi Minh memorial museum in this area later in the day.

Take the route along Ben Bach Dang and cross the bridge over the Duong Ai Quoc. Stop on the middle of the bridge and watch the hoards of cyclists teeming into the city. Retrace your steps and head along Duong L.ham Nghi towards the Ben Thanh market. Outside there are generally scores of vendors selling cigarettes, food, fruit juices, and virtually everything else you can think of. Have a walk around the market, your cyclo will wait for you. Inside you will be amazed how many luxury items you can buy including transistor radios, refrigerators, tape recorders, televisions, cameras, calculators, and many items from West Germany, Taiwan, Italy, France, Japan and the United States. In all there are 32 large markets in Ho Chi Minh, the other big ones being Binh Tay, Vuon Choi, Tan Dinh and Ba Chiey.

Continue along Duong Mang Thang Tam and turn left down Duong Xo Viet. In about 10 minutes you will cross Nguyen Trai — ask your cylco to take you to the Chinese temples in this part of China town (Cholon). This is a good time to visit because the locals often go there to pray early in the morning. Afterwards continue along this road towards the Binh Tay market in Cholon, your cyclo will know where it is. Take a break here and walk around the perishable goods area, there is an amazing array of fruits, vegetables, fish, other sea foods, Chinese herbal medicines, and virtually anything you can think of. If you are a bean curd fanatic, this is the place to buy it!

Another two hours

You will have taken two hours so far, so if you want to continue for another two hours, get your cyclo to go down Dai Lo Ngo Gia Tu to the An Quang pagoda followed by the Quoc Tu pagoda on Dai Lo Thang. From here it is quite far but well worth continuing along Dai Lo Thang to Duong Nam Ky and visiting the Vinh Nghiem — easily the best pagoda in Ho Chi Minh. It's easy to get back from here by continuing down Duong Nam Ky into Khoi Nghia, branching off at the end of the Catholic cathedral.

This cathedral on Cathedral Square is sometimes known as Notre Dame. It is an imposing masterpiece of bricks and granite designed by the architect Bouvard. The two square towers and Roman style porches are prominent features. Your cyclo can then take you back to the Doc Lap hotel down Dong Khoi or along Norodom Boulevard, named after the King of Cambodia, to the Botanical Gardens and the zoo.

Other alternatives

After a short rest, there is still plenty to see — the Tourist Authority will probably take you to all the main sightseeing areas you missed on your cyclo tour. The tourist is well catered for in Ho Chi Minh. There are 180 or so temples, the Thong Nhat Conference Hall, the old American Embassy, now an oil office, a detoxification centre for drug addicts, an exhibition of US war crimes, six orphanages where visitors can see handicrafts being made, other handicraft centres and various

The Catholic Cathedral, a famous landmark of Ho Chi Minh City.

museums. At night, it is a good idea to go and see the cultural show at the Rex Hotel where very elegant, superbly dressed girls can be seen performing the conical hat and drum dance. There is a percussion performance by The Phu Dong group, founded by Nguyen Xuan Khoat. Percussion is the music of the ancient Viet tribes and dates from prehistoric times. Instruments used by the group include bronze drums of various sizes, gongs, bells and the lithophone. Tourists may be interested to know that there are five brothers and one sister-in-law in the group. The group have performed in many countries, including USSR, Poland, Bulgaria, Hungary, Czechoslovakia and Libya. Solo performances are given with various types of traditional Vietnamese instruments. These include the Dan Tranh — a 16 string harp-like contraption, the Dan Nhi — a two string instrument remotely like a violin and Dan Bau — a monochord.

Afterwards why not splash out on a drink on the roof garden of the Rex Hotel, followed by the Rex nightclub. This is the most fashionable in Ho Chi Minh and will cost you around 3,000 dong entry. They have lovely hostesses who will charge you a few dollars for their company and hold you at arm's length when you dance the quickstep. They are strictly not in the 'hanky panky' business so watch your manners, many have been badly upset by over-amorous males just arrived from Bangkok. Remember that Vietnamese girls are very moralistic, and if crossed, are like tigers. It's worth pointing out that if you manage to get a girl back to your hotel room they can get into serious trouble with the authorities. There are plenty of Ladies of the Night in Ho Chi Minh; they say that there is no Aids problem in Vietnam but only a fool would believe it.

Tourist Facilities Ho Chi Minh City

Hotels
Tourist hotels are not up to the international standards of the West but they are improving considerably. The Rex (Ben Thanh Hotel) is undoubtedly the best, equivalent to a good second class hotel in Bangkok. The hotels in Ho Chi Minh are always fully booked — you should inform the Tourist Authority of what standard hotel you require three months in advance of arriving. Remember that mail from the West takes three or four weeks to get to Vietnam. If you are on an organised tour, you will of course be given the best accommodation available. Since everything is booked through the Tourist Authority they determine the price, which is going to vary from month to month because of the inflation in Vietnam.

Ben Thanh Hotel (Most people still call it the Rex). 141 Nguyen Hue, Ho Chi Minh City. Tel: 92185–92187–93115. Telex: 8201 HOTBT. About US$50 per night.

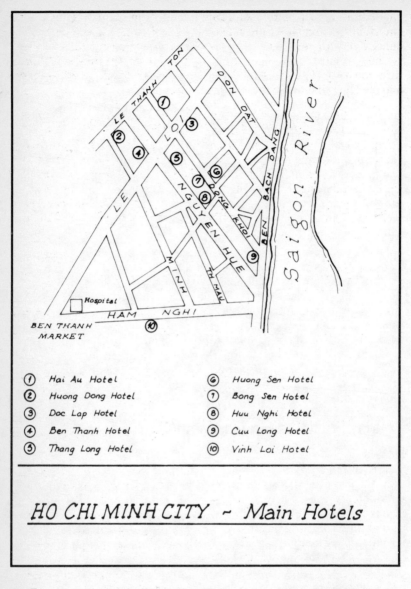

HO CHI MINH CITY ~ Main Hotels

① Hai Au Hotel   ⑥ Huong Sen Hotel

② Huong Dong Hotel   ⑦ Bong Sen Hotel

③ Doc Lap Hotel   ⑧ Huu Nghi Hotel

④ Ben Thanh Hotel   ⑨ Cuu Long Hotel

⑤ Thang Long Hotel   ⑩ Vinh Loi Hotel

It has the best facilities for the soft traveller. All 88 bedrooms have private bathrooms and air conditioning. On the ground floor there is a European and oriental food restaurant with 200 seats. There is the Apricot Flower restaurant on the 5th floor serving delicious Vietnamese food. The bar is on the same floor. The 6th floor, most of which is open, has the Peach Blossom restaurant, a sunny terrace and a swimming pool. There are facilities for laundry, sending a telex, a handicraft shop, a barber and tailor, and even a small cinema and entertaining rooms for cultural shows. The Rex is also famous for its dance hall with gorgeous hostesses. Amorous males should be warned — they are hostesses — you are now in Vietnam not Bangkok! Make sure you visit the dance hall — they play music from the 60s — pure magic! They like to charge for drinks in dollars.

Doc Lap Hotel (formerly Caravelle). 19–23 Cong Truong Lam Son, Ho Chi Minh City. Tel: 93704–93708. About US$40 per night.

This is my favourite hotel in Ho Chi Minh — the staff are really charming, many have worked there for over 20 years. From the restaurant you can look out over Dong Khoi Street towards the Catholic cathedral. It was used extensively during the Vietnam War by journalists. It has a souvenir shop near the ground floor entrance, telex facilities, and a dance on Thursday, Friday, Saturday and Sunday. Everything is moderately priced.

Huu Nghi Hotel (former Palace Hotel). 56–64 Nguyen Hue, Ho Chi Minh City. Tel: 92860–97284–94772. About US$40 per night. Types of rooms available: Deluxe – 3, Special – 11, 1st Class – 48, 2nd Class – 24, 3rd Class – 24.

Tourists on high budget tours are given the deluxe and special rooms. All rooms are air conditioned and 1st class upwards have private bathrooms.

This hotel stands out in Ho Chi Minh because of its modern design. The restaurant is one of the best in Ho Chi Minh although the service is somewhat impersonal. There is a swimming pool, souvenir shop (on the ground floor), laundry facilities, telex facilities and a dance every night except Mondays. The dance is very popular with Ho Chi Minh youngsters who flock there on their new motor scooters on Fridays and Saturdays.

Cuu Long Hotel (former Majestic). 1 Dong Khoi, Ho Chi Minh City. Tel: 95515–95510. Telex: 275 SAIGON. About US$40 per night.

There are 90 rooms: Deluxe 1–5, Deluxe 2–4, Deluxe 3–19, 1st Class — 20, 2nd Class — 18, 3rd Class — 24.

The same conditions apply to Tourists as for the Huu Nghi Hotel.

The hotel is well situated overlooking the wharf. It is interesting to get up early in the morning to watch the Tai Chi on the banks of the Saigon river. Services include bar, restaurant, laundry, conference room, souvenir shop, telex and telephone facilities.

These are the main hotels used by the Tourist Authority and are always heavily reserved. If you should arrive in Ho Chi Minh not having booked anything, you may be lucky to get accommodation in the hotels listed below. These are all in the US$20–25 per night bracket.

Very few visitors arrive in Vietnam with no booking. Occasionally westerners have found it possible to obtain a Vietnam visa in Manila and have entered as individuals; there is no reason at all why you can't do it in this way. If you just want to stay in Ho Chi Minh and not move around Vietnam, you can do so but you will find it extremely difficult to get accommodation. Try the hotels below first. If this fails, go to the Tourist Office, 49 Le Thanh Ton, Qi Ho Chi Minh City; Tel: 98914–24987, or get an interpreter from Translation Office, 205 Dong Khoi; Tel: 95515(17).

Bong Sen Hotel 115–117 Dong Khoi Street, Ho Chi Minh City. Tel: 99127–91516–20545.

Rooms are air conditioned and bar and restaurant facilities are available. They also have table tennis.

Huong Sen Hotel 70 Dong Khoi, Ho Chi Minh City. Tel: 91415–90916.

Rooms are air conditioned and there is a restaurant and bar.

Huong Duong Hotel 150 Nguyen Thi, Minh Khai, Ho Chi Minh City. Tel: 92404–92805–92405.

Rooms are air conditioned and there is a restaurant, bar and tennis court.

Thang Long Hotel (formerly Oscars). 68A Nguyen Hue, Ho Chi Minh City. Tel: 93416.

Only the special rooms have air conditioning, the others have fans. There is a small bar and restaurant.

Thien Hong Hotel (formerly Arc-En-Ciel). This is a bit out of the way in China town (Cholon). 52–56 Tan Da, Ho Chi Minh City. Tel: 52550–56924.

It's in a rather seedy area but I'm told it's perfectly safe. They have all the usual facilities but the restaurant specialises in Chinese food.

Tan Binh Hotel 201 Hoang Van Thu, Ho Chi Minh City. Tel: 44282–44026.

Has all the usual facilities but it's 5 km out of the city centre — OK for budget travellers but very inconvenient. Since it's located near Tan Son Nhat airport, it's used a lot for transit passengers.

Restaurants

All tourist hotels have European, Vietnamese and Asian cuisines. Restaurants highly recommended include:

Vinh Loi Hotel, 129–133 Ham Nghi.

As well as the peculiar foods mentioned in the hotel list, they serve excellent eels, frogs and wild game at very reasonable prices.

Thien Hong Hotel 52–56 Tan Da.

Visitors have recommended the seven course beef.

Lam Son Restaurant: Duong Tran Hung Dao — Q5.

Excellent Chinese food; the locals eat here a lot when they can afford it.

Huong Xuan Restaurant: Duong Le Loi, Q1.
I haven't been there.

Chi Tai Restaurant: Duong Vo Do Nguy, Q1.
A very crowded Chinese restaurant serving excellent food.

Dong Phat Restaurant: Duong Nguyen Cong Tru, Q1.
A Chinese restaurant very popular with the people of Ho Chi Minh City.

La Bibliotheque Restaurant 84A Nguyen Du, Q1.
Very expensive; a lot of well-heeled tourists get taken here for the French and Vietnamese cuisine.

Popular Vietnamese dishes:

Cha Gio — Spring rolls

Nem Chua (*Nem Nuong, Chao Tom*) — fermented pork (grilled meat, grilled shrimp on sugar cane).

Bo 7 Mon — Seven-course beef with special dressings — served in many Chinese restaurants.

Chanh Chua — Tamarind Soup.

Ca Loc Kho — Trout boiled with fish sauce in a bowl.

Cu Lao Soup — Assorted sliced meat, fish and chicken cooked in broth and served on a charcoal stove.

To drink — what is better than Saigon beer, and why not try *De* (glutinous liquor) or *Nang Huong* liquor.

Changing money
Foreign Trade Bank, Duong Ben Chuong Duong.
You will need your passport and currency declaration form to change money. Remember to have it stamped and keep it safe.

Many cyclo drivers will offer to change money for you on the black market. Remember this is strictly illegal. Many hotel cashiers change dollars *cash*. The rate is often better than in the bank.

Post Office: The Central Post Office, 2 Cong Xa Paris, Ho Chi Minh.
Head for the St Maria Catholic cathedral — it's directly opposite it. The post office is very French looking. It was designed by the architect Villedieu in 1886. You can send a telex from here and a telegram.

Bookshops: Foreign Language Bookshop: Duong Dong Khoi.
This is just up the road on the left walking towards the Catholic cathedral from the Doc Lap Hotel. It often has books on Vietnam in

English. It's a good place to buy a detailed map of Ho Chi Minh and Vietnam. Another bookshop, Xun Ha Saba, Duong Dong Khoi, has few books in English.

Hospital: Choray Hospital, Duong Nguyen Chi Thanh.

Airline Office: Vietnam Airlines, 27b Nguyen Dinh Chieu Street. Tel: 99980–99910.

Other useful information for tourists

Electricity and Water — 110 vols is 220 volts — 50 cycles. Warning: the voltage varies quite a bit and if you are recharging batteries, you could damage your recharger.

Water — it is purified but it is safer to drink boiled water or, even better, mineral water.

National holidays and celebrations

New Year's Day — January 1st.

Tet (Traditional New Year Festival) — first day of the new lunar year!

Anniversary of the founding of the Communist Party of Vietnam — February 3rd.

Liberation day of Saigon and South Vietnam — April 30th.

International Labour Day — May 1st.

Birth anniversary of President Ho Chi Minh — May 19th.

National Day — September 2nd.

Useful phone numbers

French Consulate General — 127 Hai Ba Trung.

German Democratic Republic Consulate General, 45 Phung Khac Khoan. — Tel: 92751.

Aeroflot Airlines. — Tel: 43774

Air France. — Tel: 41278

Offices dealing with foreigners

Foreign Affairs Service: 6 Thai Van Lung. Tel: 23032–24124.

Customs Office: 21 Ton Duc Thang. Tel: 90095(96).

Tan Son Nhat Airport: 43250–42339; International Booking Office — 116 Nguyen Hue. Tel: 92118–23848.

Visits in Ho Chi Minh City

Presidential Palace (now known as Reunification Hall)

In this area in 1868 the French built a residential palace for the

Governor called the Norodom Palace. This was to celebrate the conquest of Nam Bo. The cornerstone was laid on 23rd February 1868. The stone quarried in Bien Hoa contained coins from that period. The Geneva Agreement which put an end to French domination in Indochina in 1954 was followed by a new president being elected in South Vietnam, Ngo Dinh Diem. This palace became his headquarters until, in February 1963, it was bombed by Pham Phu Quoc, a South Vietnamese airforce officer. A new building had to be erected to replace the bombed structure. This was designed by the architect Ngo Viet Thu and named the Independence Palace. The construction took three years from 1963–1966. It was interrupted for six months because of the *coup d'état* to overthrow Diem in November 1963. The left wing of the palace was damaged on 8th April 1975 by a rebellious pilot called Nguyen Thanh Trung. On 30 April 1975 the tanks of the NLF crashed through the front gate of the palace which was the head-quarters of the South Vietnamese Government. The famous war photographer Neil Davis (NBC), who died in the attempted coup in Bangkok in September 1985, is remembered for his picture of it.

Guided tour of five storeys of Reunification Hall

Ground floor   In the Banquet Room there is a big oil painting by the architect given to President Thieu on the inauguration day of the Palace in 1967. It depicts the beautiful landscapes of Vietnam.

State chamber   This is used for big ceremonies. It was here that the presidents and vice-presidents of South Vietnam abdicated within 20 days of April 1975. These included President Nguyen Van Thieu, Vice-President Tran Van Huong, and the last President, Duong Van Minh (big Minh). Many diplomatic receptions and important confer-ences have taken place in this room. A speech by President Ho Chi Minh is framed on the back wall. In it he appeals to the Vietnamese people to struggle against the American invaders:

> 'Vietnam is one country
> Vietnam is one people
> The rivers can be drained,
> and the mountains can erode,
> but our struggle must not cease'

The cabinet   This was used for daily military briefings during the period before Liberation. At 10.30am on April 30th the 48 cabinet members were captured in this room by the invading army. Since 1975 the room has been used for press conferences.

First floor   This has the reception room of President Tran Van Huong. It is known as the Golden Room because of the colour of the furniture and curtains. On the wall, there are two lacquered paintings, one of General Tran Hung Dao who defeated the Mongols in the 13th Century, and the other of Van Mieu — the 'Temple of Literature' — the first Confucian university of Vietnam.

The reception rooms of President Thieu
Diplomatic Room: On the wall is a huge lacquered painting consisting of 40 small lacquered pieces depicting the peaceful daily life of Vietnamese people during the Le dynasty in the 15th Century. This room is used for foreign ambassadors to present credentials to the President.

Residential Area: This contains a chapel, bedroom and dining room. From the first floor visitors can see the staircase which was damaged by a bomb on the 8th April 1975.

2nd Floor: This has the reception rooms of the President's wife, a private theatre, entertaining rooms and a helicopter landing stage.

3rd Floor: Contains the dance floor. There is an excellent view over the main boulevard, April 30th, now named Le Duan after the late First Secretary of the Vietnamese Communist Party.

War Museum
In Vo Van Tan Street, this was built on the site of the Information Service Office of Saigon University. There are displays of US tanks, bulldozers, howitzers, guns, grenades and chemical weaponry. The original guillotine brought to Vietnam by the French in the early 20th Century is displayed. In late 1959 and 1960 this guillotine was dragged all over South Vietnam to execute the South Vietnamese patriots. There is a replica of the prison cells of Con Dao (the Poulo Condo island) which are known as *Chuong Cop* — tiger's cages.

Many pictures of atrocious acts of war are on display. The whole prison complex was built in the late 19th Century by the French and then taken over by the South Vietnamese Government and the US. Here hundreds of thousands of Vietnamese patriots were detained and tortured to death during the French and American wars.

The Drug Rehabilitation Centre
Address: Truong Giao Duc Lao, Duong Thang, Nien Moi.
Before 1975 the building was a Catholic seminary. It was converted in November 1975, after the war which produced several hundred thousand drug addicts. The aim of the centre is to cure the addiction and train them to do productive work.

There are normally 1,000 drug addicts in the centre at one time, aged between 25 and 45, 10% being female. The drugs that create the problems are opium smuggled in through Laos, narcotics, methadon and marijuana. Three main forms of treatment are used over an 18 month to 2 year period.   .

(1) Physical treatment where drugs are completely cut off and no substitute is allowed.
(2) Psychological treatment. Group therapy through discussions and lectures.
(3) Labour education — people are divided into small groups and trained to do productive work. The trades taught are handicraft manufacture, carpentry, agricultural techniques, food processing, and dress making for the women.

When this unit was set up it was funded by the Government but is now completely self-sufficient. Some addicts earn quite a good salary. Early in their treatment each patient is given cold showers, massage, acupuncture, daily gymnastic exercise and traditional herbal medicines.

The Vinh Nghiem Pagoda
Address: Duong Nguyen Van Troi, Quan 3, Ho Chi Minh City.
   This is the biggest and most modern Buddhist pagoda in the city. During the Ram Thang Gieng Buddhist festival which occurs on the fifteenth day of the first lunar month, it comes alive with the chanting of the monks. The construction of the pagoda began in 1964 and by 1967 it was finished. It was funded by the Buddhist Association of Vietnam. The architecture is modelled on Japanese style, the big bell and screens are Japanese made. The name Vinh means eternity, and Nghiem sacred or holy.

Chinese Temple in Nguyen Trai Street
This is situated in District 5 in Ho Chi Minh City. The temple is very ornate. On the outside there are scores of sculptured figurines on the roof depicting Chinese ancient folk tales. Inside is a statue of the Heavenly Lady who is the protector of sea travellers, and to whom the temple is dedicated. There are model ships, incense burners and statues made in China. The central figure in the main altar is Thien Hau, and to the left and right are her bodyguards.

Son Mai Lam Son lacquerware factory
Address: Duong Le Van Si, Quan Phu Nhuan. Tel: 452235.
Visitors like to go here to buy lacquerware and to see how it is made. Lacquer trees grow freely in the northern provinces of Vietnam, the lacquer is extracted and put on skilfully in many layers. Before 1931, Vietnamese lacquer was used to give a fine polish to objects of daily use (trays, boxes, wooden clogs). At the 1931 International Exhibition in Paris, Vietnamese lacquer paintings were displayed. Since then they have become as important as Japanese and Burmese lacquer paintings. When many coats have been added the surface can be painted or has various types of inlays applied. Tourists can buy any of the exhibits.

The Tunnels of Cu-Chi

Situated north west of Ho Chi Minh City these tunnels were Vietcong sanctuaries. The guerrillas used them as living quarters, stores, hospitals, and escape routes. They were only very narrow but recently a stretch has been widened to allow tourists to experience its subterranean atmosphere.

Warning: If you are badly out of condition don't attempt it; many tourists crawling on their hands and knees through the tunnels have panicked! Vietnamese tourist guides are always joking about losing tourists in the complex. It's definitely not for the faint-hearted, or anybody who suffers from heart trouble.

Tay Ninh Province

This is one of the provinces on the edge of the Mekong Delta, and can be visited from Ho Chi Minh City. Those tourists lucky enough to visit the Cao Dai temple at Tay Ninh will travel through a province steeped in history. The province in the 17th Century was still a wilderness. Fierce fighting between the Nguyen and Trinh lords took place here between 1627 and 1672. In 1838 it became an administrative division of Gia Dinh province.

The province shares 232 km with the border of Kampuchea. From April 1975 to the end of 1978, Pol Pot's black-shirted soldiers crossed over and killed many innocent people. During the French occupation and from 1967 during the American occupation this province was the scene of fierce fighting. It had been soaked with chemical defoliants but now in 1988 the war-devastated fields are returning to their former green splendour.

A huge reservoir complex has been built to irrigate its sugar cane, rubber, nuts and manioc fields. A large number of peasants who work in Tay Ninh's state farms are veterans of the war. They are upgrading their level of cultural, scientific and management education to produce huge cooperatives which work as one unit. Fishing is once again being developed along the net-work of the Vam Co Dong river.

Tourist destinations which can be requested in Tay Ninh Province

Song Boi State Farm   on the site of some of the fiercest fighting.

Mount Ba Den   (100 km from Ho Chi Minh City). From its peak visitors can gaze out on the vast expanses of the Mekong Delta. At the base of the mountain is the monument to soldiers killed in the war and further up the mountain is the monument to Thien Huong, a legendary young woman venerated by the people.

She lived at a time when the country was invaded by foreigners. Her sweetheart, Si Triet, joined the army to defend his country. While he was away she was summoned to marry a mandarin's son. Rather than do this she threw herself into a ravine. Many temples and pagodas have been erected on Mount Ba Den to worship her. The temple dedicated to Thien Huong Dien Ba is looked after by a nun, Tu Bach, who is so much loved by the people that they wonder if it is Thein Huong herself.

A good time to visit is during the Black-Lady Mountain Festival (Nui Ba Den), which takes place all through the spring season (February, March and April).

The Cao Dai Temple at Tay Ninh This is magnificently ornate and looks as if it should be in Disneyland rather than in Vietnam. The cathedral is the headquarters of the sect known as the Tam-Ky-Pho-Do, to many it is known as the 'Holy See' because of the everseeing eye painted on its front. The religion which became popular during the 1930s is dedicated to Sun Yat Sen, Ton Trung Sen, Victor Hugo and others. It is really a mixture of other religions, Christianity, Taoism, Buddhism and Confucianism.

It's best to request a visit to this temple three months before coming to Vietnam. Hardly any visitors from western countries went here in 1987 because of the withdrawal of Vietnamese troops from Kampuchea. It is now getting easier to visit but the authorities are still very particular who they allow into Tay Ninh province. If you are one of the lucky ones, then arrange to arrive around 11.30 am before the daily ceremony at 12 noon. You will get the best view of the proceedings from the balcony overlooking the interior of the cathedral. The ceremonial figures are dressed in different colours which indicate their status: Taoists wear azure gowns, Buddhists yellow gowns, and the elders are in white. The procession approaches the holy Cao Dai altar along a beautifully paved shining floor arranged on nine levels.

Part of the main altar is a huge round dome with an eye in the centre. This eye which is seen by members as emitting radiant light is the symbol of the Cao Dai religion.

Warning to Photographers: you can take pictures from the balcony but you must keep towards the sides of the cathedral. Under no circumstances are you allowed in the central avenue except opposite the main central doors where you can, if you are lucky, get a picture of the central altar. Very few photographers have ever been allowed to take a picture of the everseeing eye from a few metres in front of the altar (I was one of the lucky ones, see my book *Vietnam Now*, published by Aston Publications, England). I was not allowed to use a flash.

Ho Chi Minh to Dalat
Many tourists coming to Vietnam for the first time will visit Dalat. The Tourist Authority in Ho Chi Minh will book your accommodation and provide transport. Remember, in Vietnam foreigners are not allowed

to ride on the local buses. I have heard of foreign journalists getting away with it, but if time is a consideration, I wouldn't try it.

The journey

For the first 40 or 50 km, flat rice growing country predominates. Continuing through Borri country where the first Jesuit missionaries set out, you pass well weathered tombs some with tiles, some with plain stone. If you travel this route on a Sunday in early December, you will undoubtedly come across many wedding celebrations. After Bien Hoa, once the site of the vast Long Binh military base, there are massive rubber plantations left over from French times. Entering Lam Dong province the road is crowded with peasants threshing rice, and large lorries laden with wood, making their way down from the forests in Da Huoai district.

Lam Dong has an area of 9,933 square kilometres, a population of 396,700, with 40 persons per square kilometre. It borders Song Be and Dong Nai to the west and Thuan Hai and Phu Khanh to the east and south. Towards Bao-Loc area it invariably seems to be raining, the rainy season here lasts six months from May to October. The climate is excellent for tea growing. Visitors can arrange to visit April Tea Farm. This was named after the 30th April Liberation of Saigon in 1975. It is one of the largest in the area. Early in the year scores of school children will be seen weeding the plantations. The tea is harvested after three years' growth. If you want some good close pictures of the colourful tea harvesters, don't be afraid to walk straight into the plantation — the Manager is used to it.

The Bao Lac Mulberry and Silkworm Centre

Request to visit this. The silkworm industry has been going on in Vietnam for over a thousand years, and this is one of the biggest silkworm raising centres in the world having some 10,000 hectares for mulberry growing. New hybrid silkworms are being bred which can survive the relative cold of the highland areas. Silkworms are now raised all the year around instead of at particular seasons. If you want to visit the silkworm laboratory, you need special permission from the authorities, and this must be requested in plenty of time before arrival in Vietnam. This concern now produces 37 tons of silk a year.

The Ma Minority

Many Ma minority inhabit this area — estimates put their numbers at between 28 and 30,000. They are mostly found around the Bao Loc and Di Linh district. Many can be seen walking down the road with large stick baskets on their backs, supported by head straps. Generally, they hate being photographed. The subdivisions of the Ma people found here include Ma Xop, Ma To, Ma Hoang, Ma Krung, and Ma Ngan.

A journey through Ma country is fascinating. You stand a chance of seeing plantations of corn, pumpkins, squash, tobacco, and even cotton. They grow two rice crops a year which are harvested during July or early August and then late October or early November. Some of the Ma work in the tea and coffee plantations. Ma women are prolific weavers, they make a lively coloured cloth dyed with bark extracts. The men hunt and fish with primitive traps and spears. They use a toxic leaf extract which paralyses the fish but is not harmful to man. I am told they have some peculiar rules about marriage: it is forbidden to marry people of other minorities, a widower is allowed to marry his younger sister-in-law but not his elder sister-in-law, a widow is allowed to marry her younger brother-in-law but not her elder brother-in-law. They are married at an early age (around 15).

They have strong religious beliefs and worship Yang Hin (God of the House), Yang Koi (God of Rice) and Yang Bri (God of the Forest). Special celebrations are held at times of harvesting, funerals and birth anniversaries and even when someone is ill.

Ethnologists and photographers should be warned that it is very difficult to visit the hamlets (*bon*) of this minority. It is even difficult to get good pictures when you see them on the roadside, they invariably hurry away carrying their *Qui* baskets.

Continuing to Dalat

In the Di Linh district pineapple plantations will be seen and massive elephant grass lines the roadside. As the road continues towards Dalat, small buffalo boys ride their animals in circles on the road to thresh the rice. The K'hor tribe are found in this mountainous region of the southern Trung Bo. Their hamlets are hidden in the mountains and are not visited by westerners. They practise wet rice farming and sell other vegetables in Dalat market.

It is quite common to see K'hor people walking to the market at Dalat particularly in the very early morning. These people have many subdivisions seen in various parts of the province. These include Sre, Co Don, To La, Baja, Lat, Chil, Ta Ngau, Nop and Mang To. Each group is slightly different in their customs and traditions. The area most densely populated with K'hor is Di Linh district. In some rural parts of Lam Dong province when a marriage is proposed, bracelet offerings are made between the two families. When a person dies, some still practise the custom of putting the body in a shroud inside a hollow tree trunk. Their gods are Ndu and Yang. Many K'hor ended up in concentration camps during the US war.

Just outside Dalat, in a difficult area to get to, is a Lat hamlet. It must be pointed out to ethnologists visiting Dalat that they will not be allowed to visit it unless they have had special permission from the Social Science Research Institute in Ho Chi Minh. There is only one way of visiting these people and that is to contact Mr Trinh Chi who is an authority on the minority people of Lam Dong province: Chief of International Cooperation Department, Social Science Research Institute, 49 Xo-Viet Nghe Tinh, Ho Chi Minh City.

The approach to Dalat

Soon the road approaches pine forests containing *Pinus khasna* as the predominant species, and on to the mountain town of Dalat backed to the north and northwest by the Lang Biang mountains. This is a peaceful place, although back in the 1960s it was disturbed by Buddhist and student uprisings and suffered considerably during the Tet attack in 1968.

Dalat market.

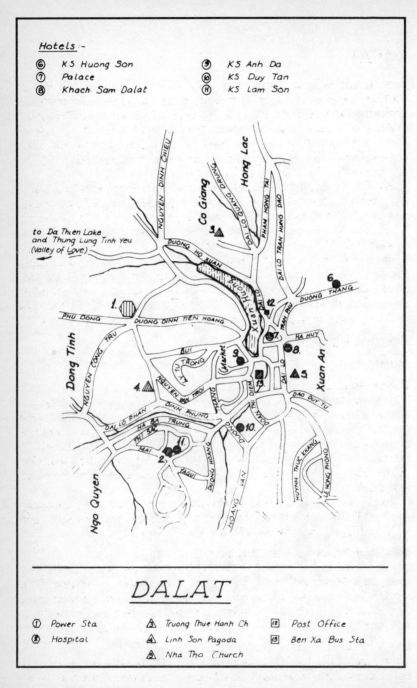

Hotels :-

⑥   KS Huong Son   ⑨   KS Anh Da
⑦   Palace   ⑩   KS Duy Tan
⑧   Khach Sam Dalat   ⑪   KS Lam Son

to Da Thien Lake
and Thung Lung Tinh Yeu
(Valley of Love)

DALAT

① Power Sta   △③ Truong Thue Hanh Ch   ⑫ Post Office
③ Hospital   △④ Linh Son Pagoda   ⑬ Ben Xa Bus Sta
                      △⑤ Nha Tho Church

DALAT

First described by a westerner in 1893, when Dr Yersin, a disciple of
Pasteur, came to the area, it is today a holiday centre especially for
honeymooners and sweethearts. Because of the cool mountain air,
Dalat is a favourite excursion from Ho Chi Minh City. The people of
Dalat are known for their natural courtesy. The name of the town
comes from Da, meaning stream, and Lat from the name of the
subdivision of the K'hor seen in the area.

From the café on the side of the central lake a prominent land mark,
the Catholic church built in 1942 stands proud. The majestic houses
and the Dalat Palace Hotel in particular remind visitors of French
times. In the distance, the tower of the multi-million dollar nuclear
reactor built through US finances dominates the landscape. This was
opened in the presence of President Diem and US Ambassador Henry
Cabot Lodge in October 1963. The town has many beautiful gardens
where European species of flowers such as geranium, poppies, hibis-
cus, roses, sunflowers, laburnum and candytuft flourish in the cool
climate. Many households have private orchid collections.

Tourist Facilities — Dalat
Hotels

Palace Hotel: 2 Tran Phu, Dalat. Tel: 2203.
The hotel has 42 rooms, 25 1st Class at around US$40 per night single,
13 2nd Class at around US$25 and 4 Deluxe at around US$40 per night
single. It has a magnificent view over the lake where you can hire a
pedal swan boat. Many courting couples from Ho Chi Minh come to
this area — a very romantic spot is the restaurant on the left hand side
of the lake. It's a peaceful place to sit out in the cool evening breeze
and drink beer.

The hotel has a restaurant, bar, billiard room, video and banqueting
room. All the rooms have extremely high ceilings, French decor, and
very inefficient showers, which date back about 40 years.

Dalat Hotel: Duong Tran Phu. Tel: 2363.
Not as grand as the Palace Hotel. It has 67 rooms, including 18 first
class and 48 second class. Prices are comparable to Palace. The
services include a bar, restaurant, laundry service, souvenir shop and a
dance every night except Mondays. I would recommend the dance, it
will remind you of the 60s — most of the music played is from that era.

Duy Tan Hotel: 83 Duy Tan. Tel: 2216.
This is generally for Vietnamese tourists. Many honeymooners stay
here. They have 40 rooms. 1st Class — 23 rooms, 2nd Class — 14

rooms, 3rd Class — 3 rooms. Services include the usual plus tennis court.

There are other Vietnamese tourist hotels in the town — Huong Son, Lam Son and Anh Da.

Other addresses

Post Office   This is on Duong Tran Phu. Just walk down the road to the right of the Palace hotel heading for the Da Lat hotel — it's on the right.

Tourist Office. On Duong Tran Phu, Thanh Pho, Dalat, Tel: 2125–2407.

Visits around Dalat

Thung Lung Tinh Yeu   This is the Valley of Love where tourists can sail on colourful sailing boats on Da Thien Lake. This lake has only been there since 1972 when the area was flooded. Young Vietnamese kids dressed up as cowboys will offer to take you for a ride in the woods where King Bao Dai used to hunt.

Excursions to see the waterfalls   This area of Lam Dong is well known for its scenic beauty. Photographers would enjoy trips to the magnificent waterfalls of Pongour, Gougah, Prenn and Camly. Camly is just on the outskirts of Dalat, Prenn only 5 km away on the road to Bao Loc and the others well within walking distance.

Nui Ba   Trekkers would enjoy the walk to the woman mountain of Nui Ba, so called because of its double peaks resembling a woman's breasts. There is a sub-alpine atmosphere and the holy waters in the area are believed to cure many ailments. According to popular belief, a goddess took up residence on the mountain in 1963.

The Ethnic Minority Museum   Ethnologists would be interested in the talk given by the keeper of the museum on the ethnic minorities in Lam Dong province. In the province the main minorities are the Ma, K'hor (and their subdivisions) — see *Journey to Dalat* — the Churu, La Oang, To Lap, Co Don, To-la, La Gia, Stieng and the many subdivisions of the M'nong including Gar, Dip, Budor, Breh and Nong.

The exhibition in the museum is very comprehensive. Photographers should be warned that everything is behind glass so forget about flash photography. There are varieties of baskets for shopping, decoration and transportation including rattan Sop baskets for containing rice. The water containers made out of dried pumpkins make interesting exhibits.

There are costumes worn by the K'hor and Ma tribes and models of their houses. Also exhibited are minority ornaments, earrings, bracelets, necklaces of silver, bronze and ivory. The larger bronze earrings are for the men. The guide tells visitors that during the period 1930–1954 the French government forced these minority tribes to hunt elephants for ivory. Some of the spears, arrows and crossbows used are on show. Very interesting is a device for scaring birds away from rice fields made out of bamboo tubes of different sizes. There are bronze gongs used in festivals, *Khen Bau* — made out of empty dried gourds — and an instrument which looks like bagpipes made out of bamboo.

The archaeology section displays tools found in the province more than 1,500 years ago. There is a statue of the Hindu goddess Uma who is the Goddess of Victory and a symbol of preservation. Rice wine containers over 2,000 years old are believed to have been used by the K'ho tribe. The ceramic vases are from the 12th to 14th Century, the pottery is Cham, and the unusual stone musical instrument is a xylophone. Read the visitors' book — it's very interesting. From the museum there is a splendid view of Dalat.

K'hor boy.

MEKONG DELTA

— Roads used by tourists   ... Rough tracks

THE MEKONG DELTA

To many tourists a journey down the Mekong river, no matter how short, will be the highlight of their visit. The traveller has to be lucky indeed to have all the Mekong provinces included in their itinerary. Most short-time visitors to Vietnam will travel from Ho Chi Minh City to Tien Giang province, where they will be given a conducted tour of My Tho, Thai Son island, a visit to Vinh Trang pagoda, and possibly taken to a snake farm. Those with a little longer itinerary may see Cuu Long province, more of the Mekong river, and a Khmer minority settlement. To see the 'real' Mekong Delta you need a three week programme solely concentrating on this area. As you can imagine, this takes a lot of arranging, special permission must be obtained from their authorities, and it will be quite expensive (about US$2,000).

In this guide the provinces in the Mekong area have been divided up to give the traveller an insight into what is available in each area. He can then, theoretically anyhow, make up his own tourist programme, and try pot luck with Vietnam Tourism. Providing it isn't too complicated, they will agree, probably with certain reservations. Don't forget to inform them of your intended programme many months before going.

When to travel

The best time to travel in the Mekong area is from January to the end of March when rainfall is minimal. The temperature range then is about 22°C to 32°C (January and February) and 24°C to 34°C (March). In April and May the rainfall gets higher and the temperature increases considerably. The humidity is extremely high in the July to October period, when the rainfall can reach 350 mm per month. Some of the provinces are badly flooded at this time and tourist travel will be severely restricted. Even during the recommended time it is wise to bring along some fast film because the skies are frequently grey.

General Information on the Mekong Delta

It is believed that colonisation of the delta area began as far back as the 16th Century. During the Angkor period, when the delta consisted of forests of massive trees and numerous marshes, wild buffalo roamed free. The first colonisers came from the sea and settled on the *giong* — silted areas where they took up fishing and fish sauce manufacture. The infiltration period during the Nguyen Lords' rule resulted in many *bung* (expanses of marshy land) being reclaimed. Networks of small canals were built which brought in silt and washed out the salt. By the end of the 18th Century two massive canals, Thoai Ha linking Long Xuyen and Rach Gia, and Vinh Te linking Chau Doc and Hatien, had been completed. The branches of the mighty Mekong river had been connected with the Gulf of Thailand.

The Mekong affects four million hectares, depositing its large supplies of silt pushed along by 500 billion cubic metres of water annually.

The visitor will be astonished to know that there are well over 100 ferries crossing the nine provinces in the Delta area. This, of course, includes all the minor ones. Major ferries include My Tho (Tien Giang Province) to Ben Tre; My Thuan to Cuu Long and on to Vinh Long; My Thuan to Sa Dec; across River Hau to Can Tho, a major centre.

The roads are well paved except in some areas towards Hatien, some areas of An Giang province, in Chau Doc area, and Rach Gia towards Cau Mau.

The massive improvements in road communication means that the markets in all provinces in the delta are linked to the numerous markets in Ho Chi Minh City. Because of the rail link with Hanoi and the newly repaired Highway Number One, the produce can easily be distributed right throughout Vietnam.

Travelling around the Mekong Delta area

The whole area is a photographer's paradise. Any of the main markets at My Tho, Vinh Long, Can Tho, Rach Gia, Long Xuyen are a sight to behold. If you manage to visit about three of them you will see a whole variety of produce being sold. This includes *Lua Canh* (non sticky rice), *Lua Thuat* (sticky rice), white and yellow maize, white and green beans, peanuts, yellow and purple sesame, sweet, waxy, pink and soft potatoes, tuberous *Cu Mai* (sweet potatoes), *Cu Tat Thu* (a kind of cassava), melons, pumpkins, cucumbers, durians, egg plants, cabbage, tobacco, pigs in conical baskets, chickens, ducks, and hundreds of varieties of fish.

The ferries are good places to meet the people. You will recognise the ice-cream seller from the bell he carries, but I wouldn't be tempted if I were you! Little girls and boys eagerly try to sell you sugar cane, pancakes, bread, water melons, plovers' eggs, rice packed in leaves, candies, cigarettes and even water. Passengers have an insatiable curiosity about foreigners — they will gladly pose for your pictures, and are thrilled when you try out your limited Vietnamese vocabulary. Children everywhere will cry out out 'Xien Xo, Xien Xo' (Russian, Russian). You will be surrounded wherever you stand, and if you seek sanctuary in your vehicle, many faces will beam in at you. The deeper you go into Mekong territory the more this applies. The whole town will come to see you in Hatien, Chau Doc, and parts of Dong Thap province. Don't be intimidated, they are extremely friendly.

Agricultural recovery

The Mekong has recovered considerably from the ravages of war, and its many other problems. Many people have told me that the rural society had been more extensively disrupted during the 30 years of US involvement than in the whole of the French period of occupation. The exploitation of the peasants in favour of the landowners has become a thing of the past. The American policy of trying to improve the peasants' methods of farming was only partly successful but has left behind certain advantages which tourists will notice when they travel through certain areas. This includes improved roads, mechanisation in agriculture and improved irrigation. But the idea of the Americans to create a capitalist-type agriculture using modern techniques to provide new national and even international resources was doomed to failure. The provinces are still far from being industrialised, and it is still a rare sight for the traveller to see tractor workshops, and even tractors in some areas.

The visitor who can compare this region with northern areas in Vietnam will notice that most people are well fed, and despite the massive increase in the Delta's population, most will have some land. Agricultural growth was stunted in the areas bombed by the Americans, thousands of peasants deserted their villages and headed for Ho Chi Minh. The chemical defoliants which were dropped affected 100,000 hectares, 45,000 hectares alone in the mangrove forest areas of Ca Mau. The lowering of the oxygen content of the water through decaying vegetation brought about catastrophic changes to the ecosystems. Through food chains the effects of the contamination spread and many areas are only just recovering. The *Rhizophora* forests providing valuable timber for houses, boats and charcoal have largely been re-established (at least in the area where tourists are taken!).

Diverse creeds and religions co-exist in Delta territory; Buddhists mingle with Catholics, Cao Dai, Hoa Hao and even Brahman. The diverse population has been mobilised for the purpose of improvement. Visitors can't help noticing how many new dykes have been rebuilt, particularly in An Giang province. The area which at one time was under water for four months now provides valuable yields of rice. Monoculture of rice is a thing of the past here as well as many other areas. Since the war new strains of rice have been developed, soya is now grown fairly extensively. The people of the Delta are strong willed and not easily deterred by hardships. Even the Pol Pot killings on border territories in 1977 and the 300,000 refugee problem created by Khymer and Vietnamese fleeing from the regime in Kampuchea has not weakened their morale.

Tourist Facilities — Tien Giang

My Tho

Hotel Ap Bac. A very small hotel where tourists hardly ever stay. It has a restaurant and laundry services. You will probably have lunch here — the food is very good.

Tourist Office: 56 Hung, Vuong, My Tho. Tel: 3154.

They will arrange excursions for you.

Tourist spots in or near My Tho

Thai Son Island   This gives first time visitors to Vietnam the opportunity of having a short boat ride (40 minutes) on the Mekong river. On the island the visitors will see a typical farm house where they will be given tea and fruit.

Warning: Wear shoes which are OK for balancing over thin bamboo bridges, a few tourists have fallen off these, much to the amusement of the locals.

Vinh Trang Pagoda   The oldest Buddhist pagoda in My Tho, built in 1848. During the war it served as a refuge for Vietcong guerrillas. There are pictures of monks who cremated themselves as a final protest against the Diem regime.

Snake Farm   This is about 12 km from the town and belongs to a pharmaceutical factory. The snakes kept here are mostly Ho Mang (*Naja naja*), Ho Da (*Ptyces mucosus*), Cap Nong (*Bongarus fasciatus*), Cap Nia (*Bongarus landidus*). These yield very precious medicinal substances. Their flesh is regarded in traditional medicine as effective against mental disorders, rheumatism, paralysis and hemiplegia. Three snakes, Ho Mang, Cap Nong and Ran Rao, when steeped in alcohol give a spirit which is an excellent tonic. Combined with other drugs, snake gall is said to be a remedy against coughs and migraine.

Don Thap Province

This is reached by the ferry crossing from My Thuan. A newly completed road now crosses the province. Highway Number 49 now links Tan An town to Moc Hoa district of Long An province, and stretches right to the Vietnam/Cambodian border. In Hong Ngu area, old people were scared stiff by their first sight of cars! The new road has considerably opened up the province, new villages have been formed, and new irrigation and land reclamation schemes have been implemented.

The new road has meant that tourists can travel for the first time through the province. The large cooperatives growing massive amounts of *tram* (cajeput — a medicinal plant), now have a method of transporting it to other areas quickly and effectively. *Tram gio*, which provides valuable oils that westerners inhale when they have a cold, is grown in the area. Intensive farming has produced double cropping of rice, winter-spring rice, and summer-autumn rice now flourishes, so avoiding the bad floods between September and November.

Visitors can now request to go to jute, *bang*, and *lac* plant cultivation centres, and to see bags, mattresses, and carpets made from them. Dong Thap is now a peaceful place but during the war it was a Vietcong stronghold, and was extensively bombed.

Other tourist attractions in Dong Thap

White stork bird reserve 45 km from Cao Lanh. The road here passes through the Thap Muoi area known for its extensive reedbeds. The scenery is magnificent particularly when the reedbeds are partly flooded in November. In February you wouldn't think you were in the same place — the beds have dried up and the greenery has disappeared. A motor boat is now used by the Tourist Authority to take visitors to the reserve. Make sure you arrange to go just before sunset or you won't see any birds at all.

The war memorial in Cao Lanh district at My Trau village. This was built in order that the people of Dong Thap who died in the war wouldn't be forgotten. The lotus petals on the memorial are the symbol of the province.

The rose garden in Sa Dec. Not many westerners would be impressed with this. It isn't really worth going to.

Mausoleum of Mr Nguyen Sinh Sac (President Ho Chi Minh's father). This is an ultra modern lotus-shaped white monstrosity built in 1975–1977. It looks out of place in the province.

Xoe Quyt district. The former head quarters of the Vietcong.

Go Quan Gung. This is in Tan Nong district and marks the position of many battles during the American war.

Go Thap archaeological site where there are remains of a town buried 1,000 years ago.

The best thing about Dong Thap is its scenery and wonderful people. What isn't on the itinerary is a trip through the small canal system — request it and see what happens!

Tourist Facilities — Dong Thap

Sa Dec
Hotel: 108/5A Hung Vuong, Thi Xa, Sa Dec, Dong Thap. Tel: 2498.
   This hotel has 80 beds, 40 rooms. The staff are delighted to welcome tourists from western countries. Up to the beginning of 1988 there had been hardly any westerners visiting this area. If you are lucky enough to get there you will be treated like a king. You will have a special banquet prepared for you, a lovely hygienic room with ultra clean sheets, good air conditioning and impeccable service. On the two occasions I have been to Dong Thap I have loved every moment of my stay.

Restaurant: Song Giang, Duong Nguyen Hue, Thi Xa, Sa Dec, Dong Thap. Tel: 2509.
The food is gorgeous, but far too much is served — they seem to think that westerners need about three times as much food as Vietnamese.

Tourist Shop: Duong Ho Xuan, Thi Xa, Sa Dec. Tel: 2509. The tourist crafts are not very inspiring — a few turtle shells, beads and ornaments, some lacquerware — not very good quality.

Hospital: Duong Lien Tinh 8, Thi Xa, Sa Dec.

Cao Lanh
Hotel: Duong Doc Binh Kieu, Thi Xa, Cao Lanh, Dong Thap. Tel: 3197.
This has 13 rooms with 27 beds. Services include restaurant, laundry, video. I don't know what it's like.

Hospital: Duong Doc Binh Kieu, Thi Xa, Cao Lanh, Dong Thap. Tel: 3114, 3108.

Post Office: Cao Lanh, Duong Nguyen Hue, Thi Xa, Cao Lanh, Dong Thap. Tel: 3349.

There is a **bank** (Ngan Hang Tinh) at Dong Thap.

Tourist Facilities — Cuu Long Province

Vinh Long
Hotel: Cuu Long Hotel, Duong 1 Thang 5, Vinh Long.
  A very small hotel having 20 air conditioned rooms. Services include bar, restaurants, laundry, souvenir shop and video.

Tourist Office: So I, Duang 1 Thang 5, Vinh Long. Tel: 2529–2595.

Tourist Spots
Tra Vinh   This is Khmer village 60 km from Vinh Long. Here you will see a Khmer temple. On the journey, visitors call at a typical Vietnamese farmhouse. An excursion on the Mekong river is also given.

Hau Giang Province
The political and cultural hub of Hau Giang province is Can Tho, it is located 168 km from Ho Chi Minh City on National Route 4. This 'western' capital of the Delta stands on the southern branch of the Mekong. It is a comparatively modern city with a riverport capable of accommodating 5,000 ton boats. In the centre of the city are wide boulevards, high-rise buildings, a big power plant, and an International Hotel. The photographer will be spellbound by the market which sells durians, mangoes, jackfruits, melons, enormous varieties of fish and shellfish. The outskirts of the city rumble with the sounds of rice-husking mills.

Tourist attractions around the area
Journey by boat run by Ship Chandler Corporation down the Hau river.

Visit to wood carving and **mat making** cooperatives.

Trip to the **pineapple factory** in Tra Noc industrial complex. The deputy directors, Nguyen Van Bay and Nguyen Van Chinh, are delighted to show western visitors around. The pineapples come from Long My and Vi Thanh and the production capacity is 5,000 tons a year. The female workers with hygienic face masks will giggle loudly as the visitor is shown around the peeling, cutting, chopping, weighing, packing and freezing areas. Foreign visitors will be interested to know that they earn about 10,000 dong a month.

Frozen Food Factory   The director, Mr Hua Thanh Hung, is pleased to have foreign guests. The visitors are given VIP treatment. The factory produces around 1,000 tons of frozen fish, prawns and shrimps yearly. It is fascinating to see the workers' smiling faces even though they work very long shifts and work very hard to peel prawns, salt, wash, freeze and pack the produce.

Can Tho University   This was founded in 1966. The biggest rice research centre in Vietnam is seen in the Agronomy department. Their main aim is to train agronomic coaches to take an active part in crop-related campaigns in provinces, districts, villages, cooperatives and state farms, and to research into the production of new strains of rice. They are making very big advances in soya production techniques to yield more vital protein, and aim to improve nitrogen fixation organism yields which in turn will give higher rice yields. They have a famous pest research team which helped get rid of the brown hopper problem in the province in 1977. They have a medical department and one which trains school teachers.

Journey to Soc Trang town   This used to be part of the province of Soc Trang but has now combined with Can Tho province to become part of Hau Giang. The journey there from Can Tho passes through Long Thanh village where the life on the canals is worth photographing. In Phung Hiep district, hundreds of small boats are rowed furiously along the Xang canal. Every day there is a teeming market at Phung Hiep.

Towards Soc Trang there are many Khmer people. It is common to see the game of *Danh Bo* where steel balls are tossed at one steel ball target. Outside Soc Trang is the Champa temple, which is highly decorated with elephants, tigers, griffins, and dancing girl statues. The chief monk (Tran Sanh) is a venerable old man. He will gladly show you around and take you for tea. He is delighted to allow foreigners to photograph the ceremony inside the temple. On the fourteenth day of the tenth lunar month there is a special occasion here called the *ghe ngo* (rowing boat festival) in which 52 oarsmen display with a 25 metre long, 200 year old Kampuchean war canoe. The 'Welcome the Moon' festival of the Khmer minority people is an occasion in which old people tell their grand-children the story of Buddha who once became a rabbit, which still appears on the moon. It is also an occasion for old people to foretell whether the coming crops will be good or not. The war canoe used in the display is a pirogue hollowed from the trunk of a Sao tree. Canoes from other villages with their own specific design carved on their side race against this canoe to the sound of a gong beater.

Afterwards at the Khmer Champa temple there is a performance of the Chxay Dam monkey dance by Khmer children.

Tourist Facilities — Can Tho, Hau Giang Province

Hotels
Quocte or International Hotel 12 Hai Ba Trung Street, Can Tho City. Tel: 20973.

This is a six storey building with 41 spacious and comfortable rooms.

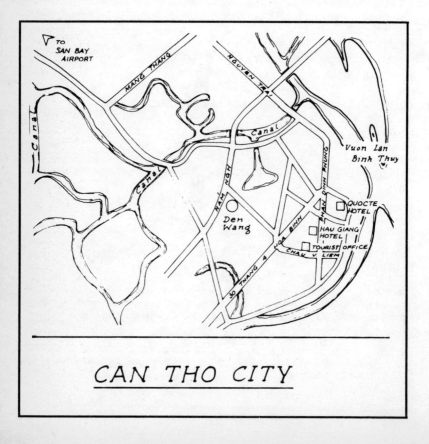

CAN THO CITY

It stands on Ninh Kieu pier by the peaceful Hau river. It has fairly modern facilities, the air conditioning generally works, there is hot and cold running water, it has three restaurants on the ground, first and sixth floors. The top floor has a ballroom and colour video cassette player. The Hotel offers both European and oriental cuisine. Try the terrapin, a delicacy in this area. It's a very comfortable hotel with a good view. Rates are around $US20 single room, $US25 double. An ordinary room with no fridge but having air conditioning and a bath will cost around US$19 double, US$15 single.

Hau Giang Hotel; 34 Nam Ky Khan Nghia, Thanh Pho, Can Tho City. Tel: 20152.

This is a small hotel more centrally situated. It has special rooms for US$22 double, US$20 single and ordinary room with shower but no sitting room or fridge for US$17 double, US$13 single.

This is a very friendly hotel — the staff really go out of their way to be polite. The food I would rate as some of the *very best* in any hotel in Vietnam. Try the *Banh Bia* after the main meal. It's a cake made out of wheat flour, mung bean, sugar, coconut milk and sugar-coated fruit.

Restaurants

I would eat in the **Hau Giang Hotel** — there's nowhere better in Can Tho. If you are here for a few days, try **Mien Tay**: 71 Nam Ky Khoi-Nghia, Thanh Pho, Can Tho, which serve good frog and freshwater fish dishes; **Song Hau Restaurant**: 2 Duong Mau Than, Thanh Pho, Can Tho City.

Other addresses

Theatre: If there is anything on, visit the Ha Giang Theatre, 85 Tran Hung Dao, Thanh Pho, Can Tho. Tel: 35528.

The cinemas, the Lao Dong and Tay Do, only have Vietnamese films.

Tourist Office: 27 Chau Van Hiem, Thanh Pho, Can Tho City. Tel: 20147, 35147, 35275.

Hospital Services: Benh Vien, Da Khoa Tinh, Hau Giang. Tel: 2007. This is the general hospital of Hau Giang province.

Tourist Facilities — Long Xuyen, An Giang Province

This is another province in the Mekong area where they have hardly ever seen western tourists. The reason is that it borders Ta Keo province in Cambodia. In the 1987–1988 period there has been a gradual withdrawal of Vietnamese troops from Cambodia so the area has been very sensitive politically. At the time of writing (October 1988), few westerners will have An Giang province approved for their programme in Vietnam.

Hotels
Long-Xuyen Hotel: 18 Nguyen Van Cung, Thi Xa, Long Xuyen, An Giang. Tel: 52927.
The Long Xuyen Hotel is very basic. All that is special about the *Special Rooms* is that they are very large with sitting room adjoining. The showers and electrical system are very unreliable — but what do you expect! It's a very remote part of Vietnam. They have a very clean restaurant and the food is delicious. I would recommend the frog. This is the hotel recommended by the Tourist Authority.

Tha Binh Hotel: 12 Nguyen Hue, Thi Xa, Long Xuyen. Tel: 52184.
This has 32 rooms with fans. The rate is very cheap, around 4,000 dong per night for a double room, 3,000 dong per night for a single. The hotel has a good restaurant and a dance hall.

Cuu Long Hotel: 35 Long Van Cu, Thi Xa, Long Xuyen. Tel: 52365.
This is very close to the hotel above. It has an even cheaper rate — about half the price of the Tha Binh. I doubt whether the tourist authority will allow you to stay there.

Tourist Office: An Giang Tourism, 17 Nguyen Van Cung, Thi Xa, Long Xuyen. Tel: 52927–52277.

Medical Facilities: Available at Benh Vien, Da Khoa Trung Am, An Giang. Tel. for medical facilities: 52989.

Excursions from Long Xuyen
Chau Doc via the Ossuary at Ba Chuc
The journey from Long Xuyen to Ba Chuc is extremely interesting. The road, which is paved in places but has some rough patches, passes many fishing villages with 'monkey bridges' (very flimsy structures made from bamboo poles) stretching across small canals. During the Vietnam War, although Long Xuyen town was left intact, the surrounding areas suffered massive devastation. This was partly due to the Vietcong stronghold of That Son (Bay Nui). The villagers of An-Chau remember well the border conflicts with Cambodia after 1975. The cooperatives in the area have expanded considerably since the trouble ceased, some now have as many as 2,000 members. The average rice yields in the area are 8 tons per hectare, most of which comes from floating rice.

Heading towards Triton district the road passes by the An-Chau village in Chau Thanh district, where the early morning market on the An-Chau canal is a photographer's paradise. A frequent sight are overloaded buses heading from Chau Doc to Long Xuyen. It is a good idea to halt here for an hour or so and watch the early morning traffic transporting melons, peanuts, sweet potato, and manioc to the market at An-Chau. Small school children will willingly pose for photographs, jumping up and down on the frail monkey bridges.

Irrigation Canal, An Giang province, Mekong Delta.

Warning: If you decide to cross one of the monkey bridges, be extra careful — they weren't designed for 'large' westerners. You will probably attract a large crowd of spectators who would love to see you fall into the canal!

Triton District

This area is a Khmer minority stonghold. During the 1977–1978 period armed Pol Pot forces infiltrated many of the Mekong provinces bordering Cambodia. Hundreds of thousands of Khmer refugees poured into Triton district fleeing from the Pol Pot regime. The drive towards Ba Chuc passes many sugar palms (*that not*). The bamboo containers slung over the shoulders of passers-by are full to the brim with sugar syrup. This is a very arid region and long irrigation canals stretching to the horizon bring in vital water for the crops. Many stretch from the massive Vinh Te canal which connects Chau Doc and Hatien in Kien Giang province. The Khmer people are instantly recognisable by their red and white chequered scarves and their darker complexions. They have built many wells because the water table in some areas is extremely low.

Ba Chuc   This village is close to the border with Cambodia. In 1978 Pol Pot's troops invaded the area and massacred 3,000 people. They sought sanctuary in the two Buddhist temples in the village, Phi Lai and Tam Buu, but were pursued by soldiers who opened fire. The walls of the temples are still blood-stained from the killings. An ossuary containing the bones, including the skulls of the massacred people, remind visitors of the barbaric massacre.

Continuing to Chau Doc   The sandy road passes rows of scoop nets on the sides of irrigation canals in Tinh Bien district. In the distance rice threshing machines scatter the stalks high into the air. After travelling 54 km from Long Xuyen, the road passes over a bridge from where there is a magnificent view of scores of scoop nets along the Vinh Te canal before entering Chau Doc.

Where to Eat   The Hoa Phung — Flamboyant Flower restaurant over the road from the temple (Chua Ba Chlia Xu) offers a very strange menu. You can have snake to start followed by frogs' legs and terrapin. The small turtles in the area are a delicacy, but it tends to put you off when they are served in their shells looking as if they have just come out of the river.

Hotel in Chau Doc   Chau Doc Hotel, 17 Doc Phu Thu, Thi Xa. Tel: 6484. It has 30 rooms, 5 with air conditioning, i.e. fan. It's very cheap, 1,500 dong/night — double room. Very, very few tourists from western countries stay here.
If you intend staying in Chau Doc to explore the Sam Buddhist mountain, the best time to come is the twenty second and twenty third days of the fourth lunar month. This corresponds to the Goddess of the Region Festival known to the Vietnamese as *Ba Chua Xu*.

Returning to Long Xuyen   A different route can be taken back via Phu Tan which is the native village of Huynh Phu So, famous leader of the Hoa Hao sect. At the time when the North Vietnam army poured into Saigon in April 1975 fierce fighting was continuing in Phu Tan. The struggle against the Hoa Hao troops continued until May 3rd when the North Vietnam army took over Phu Tan. Men in the area still have long beards and their hair tied in a bun which was the symbol of the Hoa Hao faith. Phu Tan formerly a part of Tan Chau district, Chau Doc province is an island lying between the branches of the Mekong known as the Tien and the Hau rivers. It is only 35 km from here to Long Xuyen. It is a good place to photograph the teeming life on the Vinh-An canal and the Vam Nao river.

Warning: Do not attempt to get to the area in June and July — the whole region is under about four metres of water in places!

The Hoa Hao Faith   Visitors should know something of the significance of this. The Buddhist sect known as the Hoa Hao was founded in 1939. The people chose a 'Messiah' — the prophet — Huynh Phu So. The period 1930–1940 was one of considerable hardship and when the new sect was founded it gave ordinary people hope for the future. The leader's influence spread right through to Long Xuyen, Chau Doc and Sa Dec. The French feared that the growing size of the religious movement would give them problems and imprisoned their leader in Cho Quan hospital, Saigon, in 1941. Meanwhile the influence of the 'Mad Monk' spread, and through his prophecies (*Sam Ngu*) the rich and the poor rallied together. When the Japanese invaded in March 1945, Huynh Phu So was released. Soon the Hoa Hao sect became a political organisation with a huge army. After the Mad Monk's death in 1947 the power of the sect increased until after the end of the French resistance period in 1954. President Diem, who came into power, got very little collaboration from its leaders and ordered their execution. Altars were destroyed by the President's forces. A revival period followed after Diem's overthrow in 1963. A school was set up for the popularisation of the faith and in 1970 a Hoa Hao university was founded at Long Xuyen.

A new leader, Huynh Trung Hieu, headed the sect by 1973 but because of his rebel activities, was imprisoned by the Saigon authorities.

The journey from Phu Tan to Long Xuyen   Numerous dykes are seen in the area which hold back the waters of the Hau river. This has allowed two rice crops to be grown per year. The old Than Nong canal has been tapped and irrigation water is available to everyone. Soya has been planted, and grows in mass because of improved cultivation techniques and better management. Visitors will see that in the small hamlets guava, jack fruit, grapefruit, mango, and Bong Trang flourish.

Tourist Facilities — Rach Gia, Kien Giang Province
This province is not really geared up for western visitors, very few have ever been because it's so far off the beaten track.

Hotels
1/5 Hotel (1st May Hotel), 38 Nguyen Hung Son, Thi Xa, Rach Gia, Kien Giang. Tel: 2103.

This has 18 air-conditioned rooms. The electrics are really peculiar in this hotel — the air conditioning rarely stays on for more than half an hour. The rooms are quite expensive for what they are — extremely basic, unhygienic sink, toilet with no flush. Doubles are US$26/night and singles US$20/night. They have 15 other rooms which are even more basic but they would suit the hardened traveller down to the ground because of the price US$15 doubles, US$12 singles. It must be noted that since special permission is required to visit this province the Tourist Authority fixes up your accommodation. You will need to have visited Vietnam at least 3 times before you will even get to Rach Gia, and then they will want to give you the best room in town because you're a tourist. This hotel has good food and the beer is cheap.

To Chau Hotel: 4 Le Loi, Thi Xa, Rach Gia, Kien Giang.
Has 31 rooms and 78 beds. 1st class rooms have air conditioning. The facilities are very similar to the 1/5 Hotel but the food is not as good, so I am told.

Binh Minh and **Thanh Binh** Hotels: reserved for Vietnamese tourists only.

Restaurants
The restaurants in Rach Gia are very basic affairs — short stools to sit on which aren't big enough for fat westerners (Vietnamese people think that most westerners are fat! The fatter they are, the more money they have!).

Hai Au: Ho Chi Minh Boulevard, Thi Xa, Rach Gia. Tel: 108.

Hai Yen: Hon Chong tourist centre — caters for Vietnamese tourist tastes. Excellent fish and shrimps.

Binh Minh: 14 Ham Nghi, Thi Xa, Rach Gia. This one is good for fresh-water cray fish, so the locals say.

Other addresses
Theatre: Nhan Dau, Tran Phu Boulevard, Thi Xa, Rach Gia. Very interesting to visit because I doubt whether more than a handful of westerners have ever been. The Nha Van Hoa culture house is worth trying on Ho Chi Minh Boulevard.

Hospital: Benh Vien Da Khoa, 16 Le Loi, Thi Xa, Rach Gia. Tel: 2021.

Post Office: 2 Tu Duc, Thi Xa, Rach Gia. Tel: 3402.

Central Bookshop: 26–27 Le Loi, Thi Xa, Rach Gia. They don't have any books in English. If you can read Russian they have a good selection.

Bank: Will only change dollars cash. Ngan Hang Ngoai, Thuong, Rach Gia. Also at 1 Nguyen Trai, Thi Xa, Rach Gia. Tel: 178.

Tourist Office: 12 Ly Tu Trong, Thi Xa, Rach Gia. Tel: 2081 or 2088. Get Nguyen Ngoc Bich to take you around — she's a good laugh.

Excursions from Rach Gia

The frozen shrimp factory (Nha May), Tom Dong, Lanh Xuat Khau.   This was set up and completely funded by a Norwegian company in 1979. Shrimps are obtained from the breeding station at An Minh. Permission is required from the authorities to visit this establishment. The directors Dusoh Mang and Chai Hung will be pleased and proud to show foreign visitors around.

The factory processes shrimps, prawns and fish fillets, especially red snapper. Only a small proportion end up in the markets in Ho Chi Minh City, most are exported to Australia, Hong Kong and Japan. The guide will show you the various stages in processing, shelling, sorting, grading, freezing and packaging. Take care of your camera equipment in the freezing section, don't take them into the cold store.

The Xi Nghiep Dong Tau, Kien Giang Shipyard. This establishment is government-run and produces boats from 7 to 150 tons. The 133 workers earn from 10,000 to 18,000 dong per month. Before 1981, it was used to repair boats but since 1982 it builds fishing boats some of which sell for 70 million dong. The directors, Truong Phu Kien and Tran Quoc Lap will explain the building process to visitors over a cup of tea.

It's a good idea to visit this in the early morning since you will pass the morning market on the bank of the Kien River.

Visit to Hatien

The road from Rach Gia to Hatien is fairly rough and it will take a good day with a variety of interesting stops. There are many duck farms on the Rach Gia to Hatien canal which will interest photographers. In Hon Dat district it is possible to stop at the Khmer temple.

Soc Soai Temple This is beautifully situated in a luxuriant setting surrounded by tropical vegetation. It was finished by 1970 and there are now 76 monks. The inside is slightly run down but the old fashioned decor with the primitive fan on the ceiling gives it a terrific atmosphere. The best time to visit is around 12 noon when there is generally a small ceremony.

This district is the subject of the novel *Hon Dat* written by Anh Duc in 1963. It is about the struggle of the Hon Dat people against the puppet regime and its US advisers. Visitors can wander up the Hon Dat mountain between Hon Soc and Hon Me. A grave stone at the base of the mountain has an inscription bearing the names of famous heroes, Tu Phung and Su. Su's mother is still alive and living in Hon Dat. Su had been tortured by the South Vietnamese troops but refused to betray her friends. The cave in which the guerrilla force hid from the army is now overgrown but the local people still remember how the water supply had been poisoned making life very difficult. Visitors to the area will have a very warm welcome.

Continuing to Hatien Ethnologists will be interested to know that this area contains many Khmer people. A very interesting diversion can be taken to the village of Bing An where the Khmer people process sugar-palm juice. A little further on is the temple of Chua-

Hang. The complex known as Ha I Son Tu has one monk and three nuns in residence. Inside is a statue of Sakya Mouni — the goddess of mercy, and beyond two very peculiar looking Buddhas with red lips, red nails, golden pointed hats and gold garments. The nun in attendance beats a drum while devout pilgrims pay homage.

Returning to the main Hatien road the visitor will pass the salt pits in Duong Hoa village. From here it's about 7 km to the floating bridge across to Hatien.

Tourist Facilities — Hatien

Hotels
There are four hotels in Hatien and there is nothing to choose between them. They are all geared up to take five or six people in one room. Don't expect much privacy if they are nearly full.

Hotel Tu Chau — 30 beds, **Hotel Ha Tien** — 30 beds, **Hotel Dong Ho** — 40 beds, **Hotel Phuong Thanh** — 30 beds.
All have bowls of water for washing and no air-conditioning.

When I was having a wash on the balcony of the Hatien hotel the whole town seemed to turn up to watch me. They hardly ever have Western visitors in this part of Vietnam. They hope to remedy the situation by building a new hotel near the beach in an idyllic spot.

Restaurants
There are three restaurants to choose from, restaurants in the first two hotels and the Xuan Thanh. They all serve good sea food but beer is difficult to get.

Points of interest in Hatien
The main interest is the Van Son mountain — the mountain of clouds. At Thach Dong there is a mass grave where 130 people were massacred by Pol Pot's troops on 14th March 1978. It's in My Duc village. From the grave it is possible to walk up to the Thach Dong temple inside the Van Son mountain. The inside known as Bach Van contains a statue of Sakya Mouni, the goddess of mercy. This was constructed in the 18th Century and refurbished during Ming Mang's reign and later in 1950. Sunlight enters the cave through a big hole in the roof. There is a legend that a woodcutter called Thach Sanh heard a cry for help from inside the cave and entering discovered the princess Huyen Nga who had been taken by an eagle. She was the daughter of the god of the sea — Thuy Te. He defeated the eagle and later the princess became his wife.

Hatien is also famous for its beautiful rings and bangles carved from terrapin shells. It is possible to arrange a visit to the workshops where this is carried out. Foreign visitors will definitely buy something.

Minh Hai Province

Very very few tourists have visited this area. Special tours have been run into the U Minh forest for journalists. If you are a biologist you may be able to get there through a contact in Can Tho university. The primary producers in this wilderness are the *cajeput* forests which seem to thrive in brackish water. The long light days of spring are the best times to visit, when the green swampy undergrowth grows vigorously. Massive numbers of vines twine around the many varieties of tropical tree.

The swamp is not easy to get through and any potential visitor should be warned that in places carpets of hostile vegetation may impede their progress. These are the homes of deadly snakes such as *ho mang*, *cap nia*, and *ran rao*. Many of these are collected and end up in snake farms (see section on My Tho) and are used by the pharmaceutical industry. Boas are used by the locals as a source of food and it is quite common to eat other types of snake from this swamp.

A peculiar animal often eaten in the area is *te te*, whose meat is absolutely delicious (it looks like a cross between a snake and a lizard). In the drier areas tortoises abound, sometimes weighing up to 10 kilos. Many species of birds are present but they are so shy it is difficult to get near them.

The area is recovering from Agent Orange spraying although I am told there are still barren patches. The precious cajeput is used to provide many oils such as Moi, Tram Bau, etc. Honey and royal jelly are collected from wild bee nests or from special hives which are placed at strategic positions. Some families have as many as 60 hives.

Few westerners would want to go to the area because of the malarial mosquitoes, flies, leeches and snakes, and the non-existent accommodation.

Mekong Delta

Appendices

Bibliography

Vietnam Now by John R. Jones. (Coffee table photographic book.)
Aston Publications, 1989.
Vietnam, A Complete Account of Vietnam at War by Stanley Kamow.
Penguin Books, 1983.
The Birth of Vietnam by Keith Weller Taylor.
University of California Press, 1983.
Hai Van, Life in a Vietnamese Commune by Francois Hou Tart and
Genevieve Lemercinier.
Zed Books Ltd, 1984.
Vietnam Revisited by David Dellinger.
Southend Press, Boston 1986.
The Yellow Rainmakers by Grant Evans.
Thetford Press, 1983.
Land to the Tiller in the Mekong Delta by Charles Stuart Collison.
Lanham, New York, London 1983.
Ten Times More Beautiful, The Rebuilding of Vietnam by Kathleen
Gough.
Monthly Review Press, New York 1978.
Vietnam, Nation in Revolution by William J Duiker.
Westview Press, 1983.
Vietnam After the War by Larry L Fabian.
Brooking Institution, 1968.
A Dragon Apparent, Travels in Cambodia, Laos and Vietnam by
Norman Lewis.
Eland Books, London 1982.
In the Valley of the Mekong by Matt J Menger.
St Anthony Guild Press, 1970.
Vietnam by Mary McCarthy
Weidenfeld and Nicolson, 1967.
Notes on the Cultural Life of the Democratic Republic of Vietnam by
Peter Weiss.
Calder and Boyars, London 1971.

The Rational Peasant, The Political Economy of Rural Society in Vietnam by Samuel L Popkin.
Government and Revolution in Vietnam by Dennis J Dun Cawson.
Oxford University Press, 1968.
Vietnam, The Unheard Voices by John Sommer.
Cornell University Press, 1969.
Economic Debates in Vietnam 1975–84 by Tang Teng Lang.
Institute of Southeast Asian Studies, 1985.
Vietnamese Gulag by Doan Van Toai and David Chanoff.
Simon and Schuster, New York 1986.

Published in Vietnam by Foreign Language Publishing House, Hanoi

Vietnam Geographical Data.
Hanoi from its Origins to the 19th Century.
Hanoi Guide Book.
Museum of Cham Sculpture, Danang.
The Socialist Republic of Vietnam.
Saigon from the beginnings to 1945.
Nghe Tinh — Native Province of Ho Chi Minh.
Indochina 1972–73.
South Vietnam 1954–1965.
The Ho Chi Minh Trail.
Dien Bien Phu.
Hue, Past and Present.
Southern Vietnam 1975–1985.
The Mekong Delta, Social and Economic Conditions.
Ethnic Minorities in Vietnam.
Ethnological Data, Volumes 1, 2, and 3.
Traditional Vietnam.
Nghia Binh Province.
South Vietnam.
Vietnamese Literature.
The Traditional Village.
Orchids of Scorched Forests.
The Management of Cooperatives.
Dien Bien Phu — before, during and after.
Ho Chi Minh City Tourist Guide.

Magazines

Nam, The Vietnamese Experience 1965–1975 — Orbis. Good text for those interested in the war.

Published in Hanoi

Vietnam
Vietnam Courier } both give an insight into everyday life in Vietnam.

A Summary of the Imperial Dynasties of Vietnam

This summary will prove useful when various historical facts are given throughout this book.

1. **Hong Bang Family**: 2879 BC–258 BC (2622 years)
   Kings: Duong Vuong
   Lac Long Quan
   Hung Vuong
   Name of Country: Van Lang
   Capital of Country: Vinh Phu

2. **Thuc Family**: 257 BC–208 BC (50 years)
   King: An Duong Vuong
   Name of Country: Au Lac
   Capital: Phong Khe (Co Loa — Hanoi)

3. **Thuoc Trieu** (assimilated to China) 207 BC–30 AD

4. **Trung Nu Vuong** (Trung sisters): 40–43 AD
   Capital: Me Linh (Vinh Phu)

5. **Assimilated to China**: 43–544 AD

6. **Ly and Trieu Dynasties**: 544–603 AD (58 years)
   Name of Country: Van Xuan
   Capital: Long Bien (Ha Bac)

7. **Assimilated to China for third time**: 603–939 AD (336 years)

8. **Ngo Dynasty**: 939–967 AD (28 years)
   Capital: Co Loa

9. **Dinh Dynasty**: 968–980 AD (13 years)
   Name of Country: Dai Co Viet
   Capital: Hoa Lu

10. **Le Dynasty**: 980–1009 AD (29 years)
    Capital: Hoa Lu

11. **Ly Dynasty**: 1010–1225 (215 years)
    Name of Country: Dai Viet
    Capital: Thang Long

12. **Tran Dynasty**: 1225–1400 (175 years)
    Name of Country: Dai Viet
    Capital: Thang Long

13. **Ho Dynasty**: 1400–1407 (7 years)
    Name of Country: Dai Ngu
    Capital: Tay Do (Thanh Hoa)

14. **Tran Dynasty**: 1407–1413 (7 years)

15. Vietnam was invaded by Minh Chinese and then liberated — Le Loi became King of Vietnam from 1418–1427

16. **Le Dynasty**: 1428–1527 (99 years)
    Name of Country: Dai Viet
    Capital: Dong Do (Hanoi)

17. **Mac Dynasty**: 1527–1596 (66 years)
    Capital: Dong Do (Hanoi)

18. **Le Dynasty**: 1533–1788 (255 years)
    During this period there was an interruption from 1527–1532.

19. **Tay Son Dynasty**: 1788–1802 (14 years)
    Capital: Phu Xuan (Hue)

20. **Nguyen Dynasty**: 1802–1945 (143 years)
    Name of Country: Vietnam
    Captial: Hue

N.B. From Minh Mang's reign, name of country was Dai Nam.

The 13 Kings of Nguyen Dynasty
 1. Gia Long 1802–1819
 2. Minh Mang 1820–1840
 3. Thieu Tri 1841–1847
 4. Tu Duc 1848–1883
 5. Duc Duc 1883 (3 days)
 6. Hiep Hoa 1883 (4 months)
 7. Kien Phuc 1883–1884
 8. Ham Nghi 1885
 9. Dong Khanh 1886–1888
10. Thanh Thai 1889–1907
11. Duy Tan 1907–1916
12. Khai Dinh 1916–1925
13. Bao Dai 1926–1945

Programmes offered by Vietnam Tourism, (prices 1987)

These all include accommodation, full board, domestic transportation (car, boat, airplane), entrance to Vietnamese cultural entertainment, services of guide throughout tour, pick-up at airport and departure to airport, and porterage. If you can organise a group of between 16–20 people, one person is absolutely free of charge! Remember that you cannot pay by credit card in Vietnam. The accepted currency is US dollar cash or American Express Travellers Cheques. There is a surcharge of 5% if you pay with travellers cheques. Add 30% for individual arrangements.

PROGRAMME 1 — Hanoi Only

Day 1	Arrival (Wednesday, TH 500)	TH = Thai Airways
	Hotel check-in	VN = Vietnam Airways
	City Tour	— 2 nights, 3 days
Day 2	Ho Chi Minh mausoleum	— 7–10 people US$90
	One-Pillar pagoda	— 11–15 people US$75
	Literature Temple	— 16–20 people US$65
	Co Loa citadel	Single Supplement US$12
	or Tay Phuong pagoda	
	Variety show (evening)	
Day 3	Departure (Friday, VN 831)	

PROGRAMME 2 — HANOI — HALONG — HO-CHI-MINH

Day 1	Arrival (Friday, VN 832/ Tuesday SU 541)	
	Hotel check-in	6 nights, 7 days
Day 2	Ho Chi Minh mausoleum	*Tariff*
	One-Pillar pagoda	7–10 — US$395
	Literature Temple	11–15 — US$340
	Lake of Returned Sword	16–20 — US$320
	Revolutionary museum	Single Supplement US$36
	Variety Show (evening)	
Day 3	Hanoi — Haiphong	
	City tour	
	Haiphong — Ha long	
Day 4	Halong bay (by motor-boat)	
	Return to Hanoi	

Day 5   Hanoi — Ho Chi Minh
         (by plane)
         City tour

Day 6   Thong Nhat conference hall
         War crime exhibition
         Orphanage or drug addicts'
         rehabilitation centre
         Handicraft workshop
         Variety show (evening)

Day 7   Souvenir shopping
         Departure (Thursday AF
         175/Monday SU 574)

PROGRAMME 3 — HANOI — DANANG — HUE —
HO-CHI-MINH

Day 1   Arrival (Friday VN 832/Tuesday
         SU 541)
         Hotel check-in

Day 2   Ho Chi Minh mausoleum   SU = Aeroflot
         One-Pillar pagoda   6 nights, 7 days
         Lake of Returned Sword   *Tariff*
         Co Loa citadel   7–10 people — US$395
         Variety show (evening)   11–15 people — US$340
                                      16–20 people — US$320
Day 3   Hanoi — Danang (by plane)   Single Supplement
         Cham museum   US$36
         Danang — Hue

Day 4   Boat trip on Perfume river to
         Linh Mu pagoda
         Royal palaces
         Tu Duc mausoleum — Return to
         Danang
         Marble mountains
         Sea bathing

Day 5   Danang — Ho Chi Minh (by
         plane)
         City tour

Day 6   (see programme 2)

Day 7   (see programme 2)

NOTE Programme is intended for tourists flying VN, to be extended
by 1 day in Hanoi or shortened by 1 day in Ho Chi Minh for
those flying SU.

PROGRAMME 4 — HANOI — HASONBINH — HALONG —
HANOI

Day 1	Arrival (VN, QV, SU, IF, OK, TH) Hotel check-in	QV = Lao Aviation
Day 2	Ho Chi Minh mausoleum One-Pillar pagoda Historical museum Co Loa citadel Variety show (evening)	IF = Interflug (GDR) OK — CSA (Czechoslovakia) 7 nights, 8 days *Tariff*
Day 3	Hanoi — Hoa Binh Muong village	7–10 — US$350 11–15 — US$280 16–20 — US$250
Day 4	Hoa Binh — Mai Chau Thai village Return to Hanoi	Single Supplement US$ 42
Day 5	Hanoi — Hai Phong City tour Haiphong — Ha Long	
Day 6	Ha Long bay cruise Return to Hanoi	
Day 7	Tay phuong pagoda Thay pagoda Souvenir shopping	
Day 8	Departure (VN, QV, SU, OK, TH)	

NOTE Programme extended by 1 day for tourists flying IF.

PROGRAMME 5 — HANOI — HA SON BINH — HANAMNINH
— HANOI

Day 1   Arrival (VN, QV, SU, IF)
         Hotel check-in

Day 2	Ho Chi Minh mausoleum	7 nights, 8 days
	One-Pillar pagoda	*Tariff*
	Lake of Returned Sword	7–10 — US$340
	Quan Thanh temple	11–15 — US$275
	Fine-arts museum	16–20 — US$250
	Literature Temple	Single Supplement
	Variety show (evening)	US$42

Day 3 Hanoi — Hoa Binh
       Muong village

Day 4 Hoa Binh — Mai Chau   Tourists should be
       Thai village   warned that the visit to
       Return to Hanoi   Muong village is a tour-
                                    ist rip-off. The inhabi-
Day 5 Hanoi — Nam Dinh   tants are fed up with
       Tran dynasty temple   visitors and just close up
       Tower pagoda   their doors (also applies
       Co Le pagoda   to Programme 4).

Day 6 Tam Coc cave
       Bich Dong pagoda
       Dinh — Le dynasty temple
       Return to Hanoi

Day 7 Tay Phuong pagoda
       Thay pagoda
       Souvenir shopping

Day 8 Departure (VN, QV, SU, TH)

NOTE Programme extended by 1 day for tourists flying IF

PROGRAMME 6 — HANOI — DIEN BIEN PHU — HANOI

Tourists must be warned that this tour is very difficult to operate between May and October when the rain washes away the road. Lots of tourists have been disappointed at other times as well! If this tour cannot be run, Vietnam Tourism will offer an alternative during your stay in Vietnam!

Day 1	Arrival (VN, QV, SU, IF, OK, TH)	7 nights, 8 days
	Hotel check-in	*Tariff*
		7–10 — US$355
Day 2	Ho Chi Minh mausoleum	11–15 — US$280
	One-Pillar pagoda	16–20 — US$250
	Lake of Returned Sword	Single Supplement
	Literature Temple	US$42
	Military museum	
	Variety show (evening)	

Day 3 Hanoi — Son La
Day 4 Son La — Dien Bien Phu

Day 5   Dien Bien museum
        People's Fighters Cemetery
        Hill Al
        De Castries' command post
        Trophy tank

Day 6   Return to Son La

Day 7   Son La — Ha Noi

Day 8   Souvenir shopping
        Departure (VN, QV, SU, OK,
        TH)

NOTE Programme extended by 1 day for tourists flying IF.

PROGRAMME 7 — HO CHI MINH — DALAT — NHA TRANG —
CU CHI — HO CHI MINH

Day 1	Arrival (AF 174/SU 573) Hotel check-in	7 nights, 8 days *Tariff*
Day 2	Thong Nhat conference hall War crime exhibition Orphanage or drug addicts' rehabilitation centre Handicraft workshop Variety show (evening)	7–10 — US$360 11–15 — US$285 16–20 — US$255 Single Supplement US$42 Warning: Some visitors may find the drug ad-
Day 3	Ho Chi Minh — Dalat (stop at Prenn waterfall)	dicts' rehabilitation centre distressing
Day 4	Lovers' Lane Lake Xuan Huong Shopping Dalat — Nha Trang	
Day 5	Po-Nagar tower Hon Chong rocks Offshore aquarium	
Day 6	Nha Trang — Ho Chi Minh	
Day 7	Cu Chi tunnels or Ho Chi Minh trail	
Day 8	Souvenir shopping Departure (AF 175/SU 574)	

PROGRAMME 8 — HO CHI MINH — VINH LONG — CAN THO
— VUNGTAU — HO CHI MINH

Day 1	Arrival (Monday SU 573, Thurs-day AF 174 Hotel check-in City tour	7 nights, 8 days *Tariff* 7–10 — US$345 11–15 — US$275

Day 2	Thong Nhat conference hall Thien Hau temple Cu Chi tunnels Variety show	16–20 — US$245

Day 3   Ho Chi Minh — Vinh Long
        Boat trip to orchards

Day 4   Vinh Long — Can Tho
        Orchid garden
        Freezing factory

Day 5   Military museum or Can Tho
        university
        Return to Ho Chi Minh

Day 6   Ho Chi Minh — Vung Tau
        (stop at orphanage)
        Buddhist shrines
        Sea bathing

Day 7   Return to Ho Chi Minh
        Lacquer workshop

Day 8   Souvenir shopping
        Departure (Monday SU 574,
        Thursday AF 175)

PROGRAMME 9 — HANOI — HAIPHONG — HALONG — HANOI

Day 1	Arrival (VN, QV, SU, IF, OK, TH) Dinner	7 nights, 8 days *Tariff* 7–10 — US$356
Day 2	Ho Chi Minh's Mausoleum One-Pillar Pagoda The Sword Lake The Quan Than Temple The Museum of History The Temple of Literature Variety show (evening)	11–15 — US$280 16–20 — US$250 Single Supplement US$42

Day 3   To Haiphong
        The Du Hang Pagoda
        The Hang Kenh Woollen Carpet
        Factory
        To Do Son
        Dinner and rest
        Back to Haiphong

Day 4   Haiphong to Halong Bay (by
        boat)
        Sea bathing

Day 5	Trip around the Halong Bay
Day 6	Back to Haiphong by road
	Return to Hanoi
Day 7	The remains of Co Loa Citadel
	Shopping
Day 8	Departure (VN, QV, SU, OK, TH)

NOTE Programme extended by 1 day for guests flying IF.

PROGRAMME 10 — HANOI — HALONG — DANANG — HUE — HO CHI MINH

Day 1	Arrival (Wednesday, TH 500)	8 nights, 9 days
	City Tour	*Tariff*
	Dinner	7–10 — US$520
Day 2	Ho Chi Minh's Mausoleum	11–15 — US$434
	The One-Pillar Pagoda	16–20 — US$405
	The Temple of Literature	Single Supplement
	To Halong	US$48
Day 3	The Halong Bay by boat	
	Back to Hanoi	
Day 4	The Tay Phuong Pagoda	
	The Thay Pagoda	
	Variety show (evening)	
Day 5	To Danang (by air)	
	The Museum of Cham sculpture	
	Danang — Hue	
Day 6	Boat trip on the Perfume River	
	The Thien Mu Pagoda	
	The Royal Palaces	
	Tu Duc's Mausoleum	
	Back to Danang	
	The Mounts Ngu Hanh	
	Sea bathing	
Day 7	To Ho Chi Minh City by plane	
	City tour	
Day 8	The Thong Nhat Conference Hall	
	A Display on US	
	Puppet war crimes	
	The Cu Chi guerrilla's underground tunnels	
	Variety show (evening)	
Day 9	Shopping	

PROGRAMME 11 — HANOI — DANANG — HUE — MY THO —
HO CHI MINH

Day 1	Arrival (Wednesday, TH 500) Hotel check-in City tour	8 nights, 9 days *Tariff* 7–10 — US$495
Day 2	Ho Chi Minh mausoleum One-Pillar Pagoda Lake of Returned Sword Co Loa citadel Variety show	11–15 — US$420 16–20 — US$392

Day 3   Hanoi — Danang (by plane)
           Cham museum
           Danang — Hue

Day 4   Boat trip on Perfume River to
           Linh Mu pagoda
           Royal palaces
           Tu Duc mausoleum
           Return to Danang
           Marble mountains
           Sea bathing

Day 5   Danang — Ho Chi Minh (by
           plane)
           City tour

Day 6   Thong Nhat conference hall
           War crime exhibition
           State farm
           Variety show

Day 7   Cu Chi tunnels or Ho Chi Minh
           trail

Day 8   Ho Chi Minh — My Tho
           Boat trip to orchards

Day 9   Souvenir shopping
           Departure (Thursday AF 175)

PROGRAMME 12 — HANOI — DANANG — HUE — HO CHI
MINH

Day 1   Arrival (Wednesday TH 500)   8 nights, 9 days
           Hotel check-in   *Tariff*

Day 2	Ho Chi Minh mausoleum	7–10 — US$492
	One-Pillar Pagoda	11–15 — US$416
	Lake of Returned Sword	16–20 — US$390
	Quan Thanh temple	Single Supplement
	Co Loa citadel	US$48
	Variety show	

Day 2
Ho Chi Minh mausoleum
One-Pillar Pagoda
Lake of Returned Sword
Quan Thanh temple
Co Loa citadel
Variety show

7–10 — US$492
11–15 — US$416
16–20 — US$390
Single Supplement
US$48

Day 3 Hanoi — Danang (by plane)
Cham museum
Marble mountains
Sea bathing

Day 4 Danang — Hue
Royal palaces
Tu Duc mausoleum
Khai Dinh mausoleum

Day 5 Boat trip on Perfume river to
Linh Mu pagoda and Minh Mang
mausoleum
Return to Danang

Day 6 Excursion to old town of Hoi An
or ruins of My Son

Day 7 Danang — Ho Chi Minh (by
plane)
City tour
Variety show

Day 8 Thong Nhat conference hall
War crime exhibition
Cu Chi tunnels

Day 9 Souvenir shopping
Departure (Thursday AF 175)

PROGRAMME 13 — As 12 but including VUNG TAU

13 nights, 14 days
Tariff
7–10 — US$730
11–15 — US$610
16–20 — US$560
Single Supplement
US$78

PROGRAMME 14 — HANOI — HANAMNINH — DANANG —
HUE — QUY NHON — NHA TRANG — HO CHI MINH

Day 1 Arrival (Friday, VN 832)
Dinner

13 nights, 14 days
Tariff

Day 2	Ho Chi Minh Mausoleum	7–10 — US$750
	The One-Pillar Pagoda	11–15 — US$600
	The Sword Lake	16–20 — US$560
	The Quan Thanh Temple	Single Supplement
	The Temple of Literature	US$78
	Variety show (evening)	

Day 3   Hanoi — Nam Dinh
         The Tran Kings Temple
         The Pho Minh Pagoda
         The Co Le Pagoda

Day 4   The Tam Coc Cave
         The Bich Dong Pagoda
         The Dinh and Le Dynasties
         Temple
         Back to Hanoi

Day 5   Hanoi — Danang by air
         The Museum of Cham
         Sculpture
         The Mounts of Ngu Hanh
         Sea bathing

Day 6   Danang — Hue
         The Royal Palaces
         The Mausoleums of Emperors
         Tu Duc and Khai Dinh

Day 7   Boat trip on the Perfume River
         The Thien Mu pagoda
         Minh Mang's Mausoleum
         Return to Danang

Day 8   To Quy Nhon
         Roundtown tour

Day 9   To Nha Trang
         City tour

Day 10   To Po-Nagar Cham Tower
         The Hon Chong Rocks
         The Tri Nguyen fish-breeding
         aquarium

Day 11   Nhatrang — Ho Chi Minh City

Day 12   The Thong Nhat Conference
         Hall
         A display on US
         Puppet war crimes
         A production shop of
         lacquerware
         Variety show (evening)

Day 13   The Cu Chi Guerrillas under-
          ground tunnels or the Ho Chi
          Minh Trail
Day 14   Shopping

PROGRAMME 15 — HANOI — HA SON BINH — HALONG BAY
— DANANG — HUE — QUY NHON — NHATRANG — DALAT
— VUNGTAU — MYTHO — HO CHI MINH CITY

Day 1   Arrival (Tuesday SU 541,   20 nights, 21 days
          Friday VN 832)   *Tariff*
          Hotel check-in   7–10 — US$1,000
Day 2   Ho Chi Minh mausoleum   11–15 — US$860
          The One-Pillar pagoda   16–20 — US$780
          Literature Temple   Single Supplement
          Revolutionary museum   US$120
          Lake of Returned Sword
          Variety show

Day 3   Hanoi — Mai Chau
          Thai village

Day 4   Muong village
          Return to Hanoi (stop at Tram
          Gian pagoda)

Day 5   Hanoi — Haiphong
          City tour
          Haiphong — Ha long

Day 6   Ha long bay cruise
          Return to Hanoi

Day 7   Co Loa citadel

Day 8   Hanoi — Danang (by plane)
          Cham museum
          Marble mountains
          Sea bathing

Day 9   Danang — Hue
          Royal palaces
          Tu Duc mausoleum
          Khai Dinh mausoleum

Day 10   Boat trip on Perfume river to
          Linh Mu pagoda
          Minh Mang mausoleum
          Return to Danang

Day 11   Danang — Quy Nhon)
          City tour

Day 12   Quy Nhon — Nha Trang
            City tour

Day 13   Po-Nagar tower
            Hon Chong rocks
            Offshore aquarium

Day 14   Nha Trang — Dalat
            City tour

Day 15   Lovers' Lane
            Lake Xuan Huong
            Shopping

Day 16   Dalat — Vung Tau (stop at
            Prenn waterfall)

Day 17   Buddhist shrines
            Sea bathing

Day 18   Vung Tau — Ho Chi Minh
            Variety show

Day 19   Thong Nhat conference hall
            War crime exhibition
            Co Chi tunnels

Day 20   Ho Chi Minh — My Tho Boat
            trip to orchards

Day 21   Souvenir shopping
            Departure (Monday SU 574,
            Thursday AF 175)

PROGRAMME 16

Day 1   Arrival (Tuesday SU 541,   20 nights, 21 days
            Friday VN 832)   *Tariff*
            Hotel check-in   7–10 — US$1060
                                            11–15 — US$830
Day 2   Ho Chi Minh mausoleum   16–20 — US$730
            One-Pillar Pagoda   NB It is now possible to
            Literature Temple   travel overland all the
            Revolutionary museum   way down to Ho Chi
            Lake of Returned Sword   Minh from Hanoi.
            Variety show

Day 3   Hanoi — Hao phong   You need to request it 3
            City tour   months before going to
            Hao phong — Ha long   Vietnam.

Day 4	Ha Long Bay cruise Return to Hanoi
Day 5	Co Loa citadel
Day 6	Hanoi — Cua Lo (Nghe Tinh)
Day 7	Ho Chi Minh's native village
Day 8	Cua Lo — Hue
Day 9	Royal palaces Tu Duc mausoleum Khai Dinh mausoleum
Day 10	Boat trip on Perfume river to Linh Mu pagoda Minh Mang mausoleum Hue — Danang
Day 11	Hoi An or My Son
Day 12	Cham museum Marble mountains Danang — Quy Nhon
Day 13	City tour Quy Nhon — Nha Trang
Day 14	Ponagar tower Hon Chong rocks Off-shore aquarium
Day 15	Nha Trang — Da Lat
Day 16	Lovers' Lane Lake Xuan Hong Shopping
Day 17	Dalat — Ho Chi Minh (stop at Prenn waterfall)
Day 18	Thong Nhat conference hall War crime exhibition Drug addicts' rehabilitation centre Lacquer workshop Variety show
Day 19	Cu Chi tunnels
Day 20	Ho Chi Minh — My Tho Boat trip on Mekong river

Day 21   Souvenir shopping
         Departure (Monday SY 574,
         Thursday AF 175)

Tours

Tours to Vietnam are now becoming very popular. Here is a list of the
operators worldwide that you may find useful:–

Europe

GREAT BRITAIN

Anita-Regent Holidays, 13 Small Street, Bristol, Tel: (0272) 211 711,
Telex: 44606.

1. TBN North West Travel, 92 North Gate Street, Chester CH1 2HT,
   Tel: (0244) 374915

2. Bales Tours Ltd, Bales House, Barrington Road, Dorking, Surrey
   RH4 3EJ. Tel: (0306) 885991

FRANCE

1. JET TOURS
   22 Quai de la Megisserie, 75001 Paris.

2. AKIOU
   2 Rue de la Paix, 75002 Paris. Telex: 230970F

3. LVJ
   4 et 6 Rue de Chateau Landon, 75010 Paris. Telex: LVJ 230 748F

SWITZERLAND

1. ARTOU
   8 Rue de Rive, 1204 Geneve. Telex: 427460 Artu CH Tel: 4122
   218408

2. FER NOST-REISEN (FAR EAST)
   Welchogasse 4, 8050 Zurich, Switzerland. Tel: 01 312 40 40

3. M B REISEN TRAVEL AGENCY
   Limattal STR 200, CH 8049 Zurich — Hongg. Telex: 823913 mbzh
   SBG Zurich-Hongg

4. KUONI
   Rue de Berne 7, CH 121 1 Geneve 1. Telex: 22664 Tel: 022/32 35
   35. Fax: 022/31 50 78

WEST GERMANY

SARA TOURS
Postfach 5205, D–3000 Hannover 1. Telex: 921258 Tiger d Tel:
0511–282 353

ITALY

GOING TOUR
10121 Torino, Italy. Telex: 213558 Going I Tel: (011) 517475

YUGOSLAVIA

KOMPAS JUGOSLAVIJA
151000 Ljubljana — Titova 12/11, Yugoslavia. Telex: 31463 Tel: 061
222 340

North America

USA

1. INDOCHINA CONSULTING GROUP
   844 Elda Lane, Westbury, New York 11590. Tel: 516–333–6662.
   516–872–3885

2. INTERNET ASIA (Linblad Tours)
   1341 Ocean Ave, Suite 232, Santa Monica, California 90401, USA
   Tel: (213) 822–7908

3. GO WORLD-WIDE TOURS
   San Francisco. Tel: 415–781–3388

4. MARAZUL TOURS
   New York. Tel: 212–582–9570

5. PACIFIC HEMISPHERE INTERNATIONAL
   8942 Garden Grove Blvd, Suite 220 — Garden Grove, CA 92644
   USA.

CANADA

NEW ASIA TOURS
Tour Nouvelle Asia Inc, 210 Quest Rue Chabanel, Que, Canada HZN
IG2. Telex: 4959321 Tel: (514) 384–4180 Fax: (514) 384–7045

Australia

1. INTERCONTINENTAL TRAVEL
   1st Floor, 113 Swanton Street, Melbourne 3000. Telex: AA 3065
   (ME 1228) Tel: (03) 633745

2. ORBIT TOURS
   C29 MLC Centre, Castlereagh St Level, GPO Box 3484, Sydney
   2001. Australia Telex: AA 127081 Tel: 233 3288 Cable: 'ORBIT'
   Sydney

3. INTERCONTINENT TRAVEL PTY LTD
   307 Victoria Street, Abbotsford VIC 3067, Australia. Telex: U-
   Five AA 38432 Tel: (03) 428–7849 (03) 429–8377

Asia

THAILAND

1. DIETHELM TRAVEL (The biggest operator in the world to Vietnam)
   Kian Gwan Building 11, 140/1 Wireless Road, Bangkok 10500, Thailand. Tel 255–9150, or 255–9160, or 255–9170 Fax: (662) 256–0248 or 256–0249 Telex: 81183, 21763, 22700, 22701, Dietrav TH.

2. FERGUSON AND ASSOCIATES (USA)
   426 1 Soi 10 Paholyothin Road, Bangkok 10400, Thailand. Telex: 81070 Fergusn. Tel: 271–3905 or 271–31818

3. AIR PEOPLE TOUR AND TRAVEL
   30 7 Sa La Daeng Road, Bangkok 10500. Telex: 21132 Gueth Tel: 2352668–9, 2333864 Fax: (662) 2409003

HONG KONG

1. VIETNAM TOURS
   Rm 302 Leader Commercial Building, 54 Hillwood Road, T S T K LN., Hong Kong Telex: 33061 VNTHY Tel: 3–682493, 3–676663 Fax: 852–5–766635

2. VIETNAM TOURS
   Friendship Travel, Houston Centre, 63 Mody Road, Kowloon, Hong Kong Telex: 31712 WHLTCHX Tel: 3–666862

3. SKYLION LTD
   Suite D, 11F Trust Tower, 68 Johnston Road, Wanchai, Hong Kong Telex: 66971 WSKYHX Tel: 5–8650363 Fax: (852) 5–8651306

PHILIPPINES

VIETNAM TOURS
Ground Floor, Corinthian Plaza Building, Paseo de Roxas, Makati, MM Philippines. Telex: 45013 IMEXPM Tel: 810–4391 to 94 Fax: (632) 801–1010

JAPAN

1. DISC TOURS
   3rd Floor, Grandeur Yotsuya Bldg, 2–1 Samoncho, Shinjuku-ku, Tokyo 16– Telex: DISC JJ2325172. Tel: (03) 353–2246. Fax: (03) 353–6160

2. RAINBOW TOURS
   7th Floor Crystal Building, 1–2 Kanda, Awaji-Cho, Chiyoda-ku, Tokyo 101, Japan. Telex: 2222611 IDITYOJ. Tel: (03) 253–5855. Fax: (03) 253–6819

INDEX OF PLACE NAMES
(See *Contents* for other subjects)

ALSO FROM BRADT PUBLICATIONS

Map of Vietnam   1:3,500,000
   Available late 1989.

£4.95

India by Rail   by Royston Ellis
   How to travel India's railways comfortably, cheaply, and without
hassle. Itineraries, station accommodation, great trips, steam trains.

£7.95

Trans-Siberian Rail Guide   by Robert Strauss
   Practical information on all the main routes with strip maps and
kilometre by kilometre descriptions.

£6.95

In Malaysia   by Denis Walls and Stella Martin
   The traditions, beliefs, festivals and wildlife of the Malay Peninsula
observed by a couple who lived and worked there.

£5.50

   Many other guides and maps for adventurous travellers. Write for a
catalogue to:
   Bradt Publications, 41 Nortoft Road,
   Chalfont St. Peter, Bucks. SL9 OLA